YOURS FREE!
2 Tickets (Worth $358)
To See a *Learning Annex WEALTH EXPO* Near You.

Dear Reader,

You have taken the first step in Thinking BIG and Kicking Ass by reading this book. Now you can get a shot of caffeine to jump-start your new think-big-kick-ass attitude <u>fast</u>.

It's called the *Learning Annex WEALTH EXPO*. Dozens of the world's most powerful peak performance and financial experts will spend two full days training and inspiring you to enter into the super-charged mindset of extraordinary achievers.

Two tickets normally cost $358 ($179 each)...But these two tickets are <u>yours free</u> when you purchase my book with Donald Trump, *Think Big and Kick Ass in Business and Life*, published by HarperCollins.

The *Learning Annex WEALTH EXPO* is a Boot Camp for Big Thinkers.

I absolutely believe that a sudden event in anyone's life can trigger a MASSIVE CHANGE...a gigantic attitude shift where everything is <u>different</u>, everything is <u>better</u>...and you are <u>doing the things</u> and <u>making the money</u> you've always wanted to make. I've personally seen this happen over and over again...

That is why I created the **WEALTH EXPO** and hired super-successful powerhouse peak performance speakers like **Tony Robbins**, **Donald Trump**, **George Foreman** and the stars of *The Secret* including: **Jack Canfield**, **Loral Langemeier** and **Lisa Nichols** to give you a <u>jolt of energy</u> to propel you to a new and prosperous chapter in your life. More featured speakers are added all the time!*

Accept this invitation now, and let the **Expo** <u>shake you out of your rut</u>, and motivate you to take action **now** to realize your dreams, your goals and your hopes for financial security, and the freedom to do whatever you want in life. A year from now you will look back at <u>today as the day</u> YOUR WHOLE LIFE TURNED AROUND!

All You Need to Do is Walk Through the Door and the Expo "Magic" Will Work Its Wonders on YOU!

The **Expo** will leave you exhilarated, with a new sense of purpose and determination that you have <u>never had before</u>...to start your own business, create a second income in real estate, in the stock market, in an internet business, or in one of the dozens of other business education opportunities that are proven <u>money machines</u>.

Our teachers are super-successful "millionaire makers" who will expand your horizons to a level you never thought possible!

Now it's time to take action by attending a FREE *Learning Annex WEALTH EXPO* in your area

Your first step is easy. Just register now. It costs you nothing. A Full Weekend Pass to the **WEALTH EXPO** regularly costs $179*. But you will <u>not</u> pay $179 for it...If you <u>register now</u>, you receive two Full Weekend Passes FREE, when you purchase my book with Donald Trump, *Think Big and Kick Ass in Business and Life*.

Some of what you'll learn about:

- **17 businesses you can start NOW**
- Finding, funding & selling foreclosures
- **New tax laws regarding capital gains & recapture of depreciation**
- Becoming an eBay entrepreneur
- **Strategies to improve poor credit scores**
- How to use existing IRA or 401K dollars to buy multiple properties
- **Sales secrets of the selling superstars**
- Think and be rich
- **Mortgages - Locking in the lowest rate & negotiating the best terms**

- **Legal steps necessary to protect your business and ideas**
- Identifying the right markets to invest in
- **How to invest in multiple markets across the country at the same time**
- Raising private money the fast & easy way
- **Building an instant Internet marketing plan**
- Low cost/no cost techniques to instantly get new business
- **What are the right investments?**
- How to prepare sales forecasts and financial statements
- **Real estate profits with no money down**
- And much, much more!

A New American Millionaire is Born Every 24 Seconds
Now IT'S YOUR TIME

In past years there have been people who attended the **Expo** who went on to become millionaires. Now it's YOUR TIME to experience what it's like to think bigger and live bigger than you've ever imagined. Once you get a taste of the rich life, you will _never_ want to turn back!

Call **right now** to register. _Five minutes_ is all it takes...It's a _small step_ that could make you millions. Call **1-800-488-0846** in North America or register online at ThinkBIGseminars.com

Warmly,

Bill Zanker

Bill Zanker
President/Founder
The Learning Annex
williamz@LearningAnnex.com

P.S. A Full Weekend Pass to **The Learning Annex WEALTH EXPO** regularly costs $179*. But you will **not** pay $179 for it...Two Full Weekend Passes, a $358 value, are **yours free** while supplies last. Seating is limited and available on a first-come, first-serve basis. **Register now to avoid disappointment.**

THE LEARNING ANNEX
FREE EXPO TICKET CERTIFICATE

Bill Zanker invites you and a family member to a
Learning Annex WEALTH EXPO in your area.
To register and to get more information, go to
www.ThinkBIGSeminars.com

If you prefer to talk to a representative, please call
Call **1-800-488-0846** in North America.
International callers use **646-346-2905**

Use your book receipt # _____ when you register

---

* Offer open to purchasers of Think Big and Kick Ass by Donald Trump and Bill Zanker. Original proof of purchase may be required. Pre-registration required, by going to ThinkBigSeminars.com. Seating is limited and available on first-come first-serve basis. Retail value of $358 is based on admission price at the door as of August 29, 2007. Groups may not use one book purchase for admission of more than two people. Attendees are responsible for their own travel costs. The Learning Annex may refuse admission to anyone who it believes will interfere with others' enjoyment of the program. Speakers subject to change and not all speakers in all locations. See additional rules and expiration date on website ThinkBigSeminars.com.

ALSO BY DONALD J. TRUMP

Trump 101: The Way to Success with Meredith McIver
Why We Want You to be Rich with Robert T. Kiyosaki,
  Meredith McIver, and Sharon Lechter
Trump: The Best Real Estate Advice I Ever Received
Trump: Think Like a Billionaire with Meredith McIver
Trump: How to Get Rich with Meredith McIver
Trump: The Best Golf Advice I Ever Received
Trump: The Way to the Top
The America We Deserve with Dave Shiflett
Trump: The Art of the Comeback with Kate Bohner
Trump: The Art of the Deal with Tony Schwartz

DONALD J. TRUMP

and BILL ZANKER
President/Founder
The Learning Annex

THINK
BIG
AND KICK ASS
IN BUSINESS AND LIFE

Collins
An Imprint of HarperCollinsPublishers

HarperCollins books may be purchased for educational, business, or sales promotional use. For information, please write: Special Markets Department, HarperCollins Publishers, 10 East 53rd Street, New York, NY 10022.

FIRST EDITION

Designed by Jaime Putorti

Printed on acid-free paper

Library of Congress Cataloging-in-Publication
Data is available upon request.

ISBN: 978-0-06-154783-6
ISBN-10: 0-06-154783-2

07 08 09 10 11 DIX/RRD 10 9 8 7 6 5 4 3 2 1

CONTENTS

CONTENTS

5

FEAR FACTOR   137

6

REVENGE   177

7

BIG MO!   201

8

NEVER TAKE YOUR EYE OFF THE BALL   225

9

I LOVE YOU, SIGN THIS   249

10

THINK BIG AND KICK ASS IN BUSINESS AND LIFE   265

APPENDIX

FOREWORD

Throughout my years in business there have been certain people who have left an indelible impression. Bill Zanker is one of those people. When I first met him, I realized he was not only a very intelligent and dynamic person, but a dynamo in every sense of the word. I found myself enjoying his ideas and his enthusiasm.

Creativity is an important element of success, no matter what your business might be. Bill has that creativity and he knows how to put it into action. Anyone who has been around Bill will never forget him. He's a gifted promoter and his positive outlook has affected many thousands of people on a most productive level. He's an educator who also knows and fully understands his subject.

He also loves his business, which is one of my prerequisites when talking about success. His passion for his work remains undiminished and The Learning Annex has unfolded in a remarkable way.

Think Big is a credo that I have embraced since my youth, and it has proven to be an effective way to achieve success. Bill has also employed this attitude and the results are evident. Writing this book together has been a "kick ass" experience for both of us—and we hope you will not only enjoy the results, but learn a lot at the same time. We're hoping to see all of you achieve your biggest dreams—and if you work hard, you will!

Donald J. Trump

THINK
BIG

AND KICK ASS

IN BUSINESS AND LIFE

INTRODUCTION

FROM SMALL TO BIG

The Learning Annex was a small company until I met Donald Trump. Now it is a large company because I mastered Donald Trump's kick-ass attitude. About twenty-eight years ago, when I was a student taking film courses at The New School in New York City, I needed to make some money to support myself. So in 1979, at age twenty-six, I took the $5,000 I had gotten from my bar mitzvah and used it to start The Learning Annex. At first I thought of it as an informal school for experimental film instructors to share their knowledge with aspiring filmmakers. But my girlfriend at the time, a pottery teacher, talked me into expanding the curriculum and making a school for a different way of learning, a way for people to get a quick education about things they could not learn elsewhere. The Learning Annex was born.

In those early days I would dress up in a clown's costume and stand on the streets of Manhattan handing out course catalogs. I would tell people to call the office number in the catalog and say the clown told them to register to save five dollars on the class. Then I would run to the office and answer the calls. And to my excitement, loads of calls came in from people telling me a nice clown had told them about a discount. I would sign up each student for the class and send out the class confirmation letter. When there were no calls, I would look for new teachers to speak. I was a business of one and running it out of my $325-a-month studio apartment on the Upper West Side of Manhattan.

My film career never took off, but The Learning Annex did, and I loved it. I realized I was a born promoter and I had found my passion.

I changed the whole concept of continuing education to what I call "edu-tainment." Everything is quick these days. Nobody has time for education. MTV and the Internet have created a generation of people who want everything to be fast-

paced and entertaining. I decided to go after big-name personalities and celebrities to teach the classes. I wanted the teachers
to have big personalities and to be larger than life.

When we added the glamour of celebrity names to our
roster, attendance skyrocketed, and more and more luminaries
were willing to say yes to my requests for them to teach. Sarah
Jessica Parker, Harrison Ford, Richard Simmons, Henry
Kissinger, P. Diddy, Suze Orman, Barbara Bush, Larry King,
Desmond Tutu, Renee Zellweger, Deepak Chopra, and Rudy
Giuliani have graced the podium of The Learning Annex, along
with hundreds of others.

How did I lasso these stars? Since I did not have a lot of
money, I got celebrities by using a different appeal: guilt. I
would say, "You've made it big. Why don't you give back to
society?" I remember movie mogul Harvey Weinstein. He was
an extremely tough cookie to get. I whined and whined and
whined at him, "You can give Learning Annex students an hour
of your time for charity." He finally did it, and he was amazing
at telling the most fascinating insights on how to break into
Hollywood. And he ended up speaking for several hours. Same
with legendary record producer Clive Davis; not only did he
listen to students' demos, he signed someone right there during
the class. For most of these luminaries the money was irrelevant anyway.

Except for Donald Trump. He would not even take my

calls. One day I called Trump's office and was put through to his personal secretary Norma. I knew I could not get Trump's attention using my usual pitch. He would not even talk to me. So I had to do something different to get his attention. I decided to pique his interest with money, which is extremely unusual for me. But I really wanted to get him, so I decided to go for it. I offered what to me was an enormous amount of money: $10,000. His secretary asked, "That's it?" and dismissed my offer as if it were a cheap bottle of Chianti. She curtly added, "I don't think so" and hung up the phone.

It took a lot of courage but a few days later, undaunted, I called Norma again and said, "I'll give Mr. Trump twenty-five thousand dollars." Norma said, "Nope. He's not interested." I was stunned. After that I realized I had been playing it safe. The following week I took an enormous risk; I offered $100,000. That was the most money I had ever offered a speaker, but it had no impact on Norma, who said without hesitation, "No way. Donald still couldn't do it."

I sat back and thought really hard about what to do next. Should I drop the idea of having Donald Trump, or should I keep trying? I did not know what to do. Then I remembered what performance guru Tony Robbins had taught me, "If you want to make it big, you've got to push yourself beyond your limits. You've got to pump yourself up and get yourself into a hyper mental state. And you have to do this yourself. Nobody can do this for you." I decided I wanted to be big. Donald Trump was the ultimate Mr. Big. We all have heroes, and Donald was mine. If I wanted to play in the same arena as him, I had to push myself to a new level. I pushed out my chest, took a deep breath, and gathered all the energy I could muster. Then I called Norma at Donald Trump's office and offered one million dollars for Trump to speak for one hour at The Learning Annex. At the time, The Learning Annex had never grossed more than $5.5 million in an entire year. Think about it, I offered him a million dollars, and I was only bringing in $5.5 million a year. And I had rarely had a class of more than a few hundred students. How I was going to get my money back was beyond me at that moment. But I knew I had to do it. I just knew it. So I listened to my gut and made the call. And Norma said, "That's very interesting. I'll talk to Donald about it."

I hung up the phone, went into the bathroom, and promptly threw up. *Really.* My mind was racing, and my heart was pounding. What had I done? If it did not work out, I could lose everything! In one minute I had gone to a whole new level in my life, and it was very uncomfortable. But it was also exhilarating! What I had just done was insane. But it felt great.

In less than one hour, Donald called me back himself.

When I picked up the phone I could hardly believe I was talking with Donald Trump. I thought maybe it was a friend goofing on me. But it was Donald. He said, "Bill, I like The Learning Annex, and you made me a very nice offer. Let me ask you, how many people are you going to get for this event?" Up until then most of our classes had between 500 and 700 people, and the biggest class had been for a psychic. We had never had more than several hundred students for any of our events. So I told him, "I'll get one thousand people." In my mind, 1,000 people was a huge number of people. Trump retorted, "I'll do it if you can promise me you'll get ten thousand people."

Ten thousand people! I had never imagined getting 10,000 people in my wildest dreams. But I boldly said, "Yes. I'll get ten thousand people. No problem." Trump said, "Great. My lawyer will send over the paperwork." And that was it. The deal was done. By saying "yes" I had made a solid commitment to living very big, bigger than ever before. That moment changed my life. Donald Trump took me to a whole new level. I started doing things I had never done before. I started thinking on a much larger scale. I had to get 10,000 people to come see Donald Trump. And guess what? Everyone wanted to learn from Donald, and the registrations started flying in.

That is how The Learning Annex Wealth Expo came about. As it turned out, I got much more than the 10,000 people I promised Trump. Over 31,500 people attended our first Learning Annex Wealth Expo in 2004. It was an amazing turnout. And as a result, it was actually very easy to pay Donald Trump his fee. Trump knew all along that I could do it. I thank him for challenging me to change the way I think. The experience proved to me beyond any doubt that when you think big, big things come to you. My company has grown over 400 percent every year since I met Donald Trump, zooming from a small company earning $5.5 million in sales to a big company making $102 million last year. The Learning Annex was named one of *Inc.* magazine's fastest growing companies two years in a row. All because I learned the Think BIG and Kick Ass principles that you will read about in this book.

Working with Donald Trump has completely changed the way I think. I had heard the term "think big," but I never really understood it. Thinking big is a way of life for Donald Trump. I learned from him that to really think big you must discard the comforts of your own insecurities. I learned that to be successful you must never give up. Every failure is a step on the way to success. Donald Trump has a can-do, take-no-prisoners attitude. Be your own person. Demand what you want in life. Do not let other people run your life. Do not let people push you around. If someone crosses you, do not lie down and take it; fight back, kick ass, and get even. Make your own rules, and do not care what other people think. That is what Donald Trump is all about. Through his attitude and his example Donald Trump has taught me how to truly think big. And now I live a life of much bigger energy, much bigger goals, and much bigger income.

My new attitude has boosted my self-confidence enormously. I have no trouble making big plans and going after top-name celebrities, whether it is Warren Buffett, Rupert Murdoch, or even President Clinton. Nothing scares me anymore. My business life and my personal life have been transformed by my friendship with Donald Trump. I am a much better man who believes in himself. I have become a millionaire many times over. I value myself more, and that has filtered into my personal life as well. I am a better husband to my wife and a better father to my children. My wife loves my new attitude, and my kids respect the new me. Their lives have also been transformed. After seeing crowds of 50,000 people, my son Dylan has become more interested in business. After listening to Donald Trump, my daughters Ediva and Vera have pursued their lives with more passion. My wife, Debbie, admires the risks I take and supports me in my business ventures. If you are a small business owner, it is very important that you get support from your spouse. Just knowing that my wife is behind me helps me when I get scared. Running a small business has risks; it is a battle, and it is important that your spouse and children are with you in this battle.

I was working 24/7 in the days leading up to our first Wealth Expo in New York City in 2004. At 4 A.M. the morning of the expo, I was in a 24-hour deli nearby the Jacob K. Javits Convention Center, buying a birthday cake for one of the guys on the team. He was giving up his birthday to do the expo, so that was the least I could do. I got a call from Harry Javer, who was running the expo. He said "Get your ass down here now. We have a major problem. We have lines of people blocking the doors. The Javits Center is going insane. They have never seen lines like this before, and at 4 A.M.!"

When we did that first mega-expo in 2004 we had no idea what we were getting into. If we had told somebody that we were going to attract 30,000-plus people at our first show, they would have said it was impossible. As a matter of fact, most "experts" said we would not even get 5,000 people. Since we did not have experience with huge shows, we did not know any better. That first morning the lines to get into the Javits Center were eight blocks long. We had spent a huge amount of money promoting the event. Everybody wanted to meet Donald and learn his secrets. The promotion paid off: the crowds came. It was an entrepreneur's dream come true. I had bet big, and I won. I was now a big believer in Donald's Think Big strategies.

After the first expo The Learning Annex did more Wealth Expos with Donald Trump, and they were amazing. In San Francisco over 70,000 attended and two weeks later in Los Angeles 62,500 people came. It was an extraordinary ride. Everything was going great. So I called Trump and said I wanted to sign him up for the following year to do up to twenty shows. He said, "Great. But all these people are coming because of me. I want a raise." I said, "No, Mr. Trump. I worked very hard and I did all the advertising. That's why it worked." He said, "Nonsense. It's because of me. I now want one and a half million dollars." And you know what? I agreed, because he deserved it. He was changing my life and my students' lives.

That is an example of the Trump attitude. Trump knows his worth, and he gets people to pay him for it. But it is not only for the money. With Trump it is never just for the money. He is passionate about everything he does. He loves connecting with people, helping them, and educating them. If you consider the advertising, promotions, and everything The Learning Annex does to enhance the Trump brand, nationally and internationally, Donald gets much more than $1.5 million per speech—but he donates much of the money to charity.

Donald Trump is tough. Donald Trump is demanding. And Donald Trump commands top dollar. But surprisingly, he is the easiest guy in the world to work with. And I work with a lot of celebrities. He is always professional and always prepared. He always overdelivers by giving my students and me more than I expected and more than he was required to do. And he is one of the most loyal guys in the world. Loyalty is important to Trump and is a wonderful trait to have in business.

Donald Trump wants to share his successful attitude with more people. He knows how to give back. He teaches the way people taught hundreds of years ago, through stories. This book is about what really matters—the *attitude* of thinking big, based on real-life anecdotes. As you read, take a moment and think about the stories. I guarantee that, like the hundreds of students who have written to me, when a situation comes up in your *own* life, you will remember a Trump story and how he dealt with it. It will make you deal with your own situation differently. That is why this book is so important. Read it. Enjoy it. And without you even realizing it, this book will change your attitude and your life. I guarantee it.

Read each chapter, and let the Trump attitude sink in and teach you a lesson. Adapt Trump's bold, kick-ass attitude to fit your life. Use the Trump attitude to inspire you to break through the limits you have set for yourself. You always have two options in life: you can think small or you can think big. As Trump says, "If you're thinking already, you might as well think big. It is your choice. No matter what your circumstances, nobody can stop you from thinking big." Once you get a taste of thinking big and learn the kick-ass way, you will never want to stop, and the rich rewards will come to you. It is Donald's secret of thinking big and kicking ass; practice it and you too will be prosperous in business and life.

I love and respect Donald Trump. He has changed my business, personal, and financial life. I am indebted to him, and I am so pleased to be sharing his teachings with you. I guarantee it will make a shift in your life as it has in mine and in those of my students.

Thank you, Donald, for teaching me the secret of Thinking BIG and Kicking Ass.

—Bill Zanker, President / Founder, The Learning Annex

1

DO YOU HAVE WHAT IT TAKES?

People always ask me, "How did you get so rich?" The way I do things has allowed me to succeed financially far beyond what I had expected. I have had a lot of fun, and I have made a lot of money. I have known many celebrities, billionaire businesspeople, and superstar sports figures. It is not easy to explain in a couple of words, but I have noticed that all these successful people have traits that set them apart from the pack: their attitudes, actions, persistence, and passion, plus a whole slew of other qualities that separate the winners from the losers.

To be successful you have to separate yourself from 98 percent of the rest of the world. Sure, you can get into that special 2 percent at the top, and it is not just by being smart, working hard, and investing wisely. There is a formula, a recipe for success that the top 2 percent live by and that you too can follow to be successful.

First, you must be honest with yourself. The only way to get rich is to be realistic and brutally honest. You have to get out of the ideal fantasy world you read about in magazines and see on TV. It is not as easy as they make it look. It is tough, and people get hurt. So you have to be as tough as nails and willing to kick ass if you want to win. Most people are not cut out for this. You have to deal with a tremendous amount of pressure. You have to think large and be creative to solve big problems that scare the crap out of most people. People are going to try to steal from you and destroy you just for the fun of it. You have to stand up to them, fight back and kick their ass. Nobody is going to hold your hand and help you along. You are on your own. You have to be able to bend but never break.

All of the greats in every sport, in finance and business, in the arts, and in government possess something special. A lot of people have it, but frankly, most people do not. Do you have what it takes to think big and kick ass? Virtually all self-made millionaires and billionaires, such as Bill Gates, Oprah Winfrey, and Walt Disney had the ability to think big and kick ass. It is hard to explain, so I have devised the following success quiz, which you can take to see if you have it. If you have it, you are going to make a lot of money.

Take this quiz to see if you match the profile:

1. How much money do you want to have in five years?

    a. $100,000 to $249,999.

    b. $250,000 to $499,999.

    c. $500,000 to $4,999,999.

    d. $5 million or more.

2. What is your financial dream?

    a. Winning the lottery.

    b. Getting a good job with health benefits, a 401(k), and three weeks vacation.

    c. Owning my own home.

    d. Having unlimited passive income from a business and/or real estate holdings or other investments.

3. Which statement best describes your financial situation?

    a. I am very satisfied with where I am financially.

    b. I am somewhat satisfied with where I am financially.

    c. I am unsatisfied but feel hopeless.

    d. My financial situation is completely unsatisfactory. I want much more.

4. How much time do you spend each day building your wealth?

    a. Less than half an hour.

    b. Half an hour to one hour.

c. One hour to two hours.

d. Two hours or more.

5. How much money do you spend on business, financial education, and training?

    a. Less than $100 per year.

    b. $100 to $499 per year.

    c. $500 to $1,199 per year.

    d. More than $1,200 per year.

6. What do you do when you are faced with a difficult problem?

    a. Ignore it and hope it will go away.

    b. Complain to my friends and family.

    c. Turn it over to someone else to worry about.

    d. Brainstorm until I find a creative solution.

7. What is your attitude toward work?

    a. It is drudgery. I hate my job.

    b. I do not mind work, but I wish I were doing something else.

    c. Work is okay. I have to work to get paid.

    d. I love to work. It is exhilarating and fun.

8. What would you do if you lost your job or source of income?

    a. Save money by moving in with friends or family and collect unemployment insurance.

    b. Go back to school for retraining.

    c. Find a new job.

    d. Start my own company.

9. Which statement best describes your energy and concentration level?

    a. I barely have enough energy to get through the day.

    b. I work hard for a while, and then I run out of steam and coast through the rest of the day.

    c. I can work hard for eight hours.

    d. I am a blaze of energy, and I never get tired when I am doing something I enjoy.

10. Which best describes your reaction when someone tells you that you can't do something?

    a. I give up and sit around feeling sorry for myself.

    b. I lose my temper and throw a tantrum.

    c. I give it another try.

    d. I get energized, and will not give up until I get what I want.

11. You have an important decision to make and you do not know what to do. Which statement best describes your decision-making process?

   a. I watch a lot of TV.

   b. I talk to all my friends to see what they would do.

   c. I analyze the situation logically and do what seems to make the most sense.

   d. I trust my gut instincts after doing b and c.

12. What is your attitude toward people?

   a. I believe people are generally good and would never lie, cheat, or steal from me.

   b. I surround myself with people who look up to me, even if they are not the best qualified.

   c. I hire the best people and trust them to do a good job.

   d. I hire the best people and treat them professionally, but I watch them like a hawk.

13. When someone intentionally harms you or your reputation, how do you react?

   a. I get very depressed and wonder why they do not like me.

   b. I let it go. Why cause a stir?

c. I confront them and ask them why they did what they did.

d. I strike back, doing the same thing to them only ten times worse.

14. You are "on a roll" and everything seems to be going your way. What do you do now?

a. Take time off to go on vacation.

b. Maintain the status quo.

c. Start dabbling in another business or another career.

d. Stay involved and focused on my main business or career, driving it to new heights.

15. What is your attitude toward the business of being in a marriage?

a. My spouse and I love each other, and we would never get a divorce.

b. I believe my spouse loves me and even if we split, things would end amicably.

c. Divorce is a possibility. I do not want to think about it now.

d. I love my spouse, and I do not want it to end, but I signed a prenuptial agreement to protect my finances in case it does.

Now, tally up your score. Count up the number of a's, b's, c's, and d's. Give yourself 1 point for every a, 2 points for every b, 3 points for every c, and 4 points for every d. Read the chart below to see how you rate.

NUMBER OF POINTS	HOW YOU RATE
15–25	Poor. You need a major attitude overhaul.
26–35	Average. You need to kick-start your attitude into high gear.
36–45	Good. You have potential but need to improve.
46–60	Excellent. You are ready for the big leagues. Let it rip!

EXPLANATIONS OF THE QUESTIONS:

1. *How much money do you want to have in five years?*

If you chose the lowest amount, why did you do that? You have a choice of getting any amount from $100,000 to $5 million in the next five years. It is completely up to you. Nobody is telling you what to choose. So why would anyone choose $100,000?

Yet in life that is exactly what many people do. They settle for $100,000 when they could just as easily have $5 million. Choosing less money shows a lack of ambition and a lack of confidence. Do not start out by settling. Always shoot for the top. Every great athlete and every great billionaire goes for the gold, not the bronze. If it were me answering this question, I would scratch out *$5 million* and write in *$50 billion*! That is the attitude you must have to make it big.

2. *What are your financial dreams?*

What you dream about is what you will do. If you cannot even dream of doing big things, you will never do anything big in life. I spent my first few weeks in Manhattan dreaming of what I would do with a huge piece of vacant real estate on New York's West Side that was owned by the bankrupt Pennsylvania and New York Central Transportation Company. After eighteen months of hard work and focus, I took an option to the property, worth $62 million, *with no money down*. I conceived the Javits Center on the land. That is the power of big dreams. What kind of big dreams excite you and make you feel great? Do not worry about whether you can do it. That does not matter. It does not cost anything to dream. Spend your time enjoying your big dreams.

DONALD J. TRUMP AND BILL ZANKER

3. *Which statement best describes your financial situation?*

This question shows how hungry you are. Hungry people work harder and are much more motivated to make great strides forward in life. If you are satisfied with your current financial situation, what is going to motivate you to do all the things you need to do to become rich and successful? You have to set higher and higher goals. You have to want more or you will start slipping backwards fast.

4. *How much time do you spend each day building your wealth?*

Wealth comes from big goals and sustained action toward those goals every day. Many people start with big goals. Yet after they run into a few problems or get distracted by other things that compete for their attention every day, they lose focus on their goals. To keep your goals alive you must take action every single day for at least two hours. No one should care about your money and success more than you do.

5. *How much money do you spend on business, financial education, and training?*

Finance and business are dangerous waters where vicious sharks are swimming around looking to feed on innocent novices. In this game, knowledge is the key to power. Spend the money necessary to know what you are doing or somebody will quickly be doing you. Financial illiteracy is a huge problem in this country. People get trapped in very bad situations because they did not do their homework.

6. *What do you do when you are faced with a difficult problem?*

Rich people are rich because they solve difficult problems. You must learn to thrive on problems. CEOs of big companies are paid huge amounts of money because they solve problems that nobody else can solve. Some are good at what they do and some are terrible and overpaid. I face problems every day. It is one of the things I do best. If you want to be in the top 2 percent, you must become very good at finding creative solutions to what appear to be impossible problems.

7. *What is your attitude toward work?*

There is no worse feeling than being trapped in a job you do not enjoy. You have to love what you do. To be a success the most important thing is to love what you do. You have to put in long hours and face enormous challenges to be successful. If you do not love what you do, you will never make it through. If you love your work, the difficulties will be balanced out by the enjoyment. I love making deals and constructing great buildings. The fun I am having every day keeps me going when things get tough.

8. *What would you do if you lost your job or source of income?*

This is the ultimate test. If disaster struck, would you fold up and go home to your mother? Or would you pick yourself up and make something happen? The biggest doers often suffer the biggest setbacks in life. So if you want to aim high, you have to have the guts to handle the inevitable bumps in the road. If you strike out, nobody is going to help you—not your friends, not the government. You have to look out for yourself, and your attitude is the key to surviving a setback. Look at shoe maven Steve Madden: he had some legal trouble, but he had a successful attitude that could not be subdued, and he staged a big-time comeback. You have to know that you have what it takes to come back from anything. Martha Stewart is another example—what a great and brave comeback she made—few people could have done what she did!

9. *Which statement best describes your energy and concentration level?*

In truth you have more energy than you think you have. Most people are working at about 50 percent capacity. You can do much more. It takes a crisis or an emergency to get most people up to full steam. I get charged up by loving what I do. Nothing is more important to me than the excitement of putting caution to the wind and doing something that has never been done before. I love the thrill of jumping headfirst into a big challenge, and then using all of my talents to make it successful. Passion is why Mark Burnett, Jim Cramer, and Arnold Schwarzenegger are at the tops of their fields. All successful people are high-energy people who are passionate about what they do. Find a passion that energizes you!

10. *Which best describes your reaction when someone tells you that you cannot do something?*

If you want to be a success, you have to get used to frequently hearing the word *no* and ignoring it. As a child, when your mother told you no, your father told you no, the teacher told you no, or the coach told you no, if you were a good little boy or girl, you listened to the word *no* and stopped what you were doing. That is why 98 percent of adults are conditioned to stop when they hear the word *no*. Quitters do not get anywhere. You will not be successful if you listen to nos.

If you want to be in the top 2 percent, you have to get real. In business you are not dealing with your mother, your father, or your teacher. People are not looking out for you. They do not want the best for you; they are looking out for themselves.

When most people say no, they are doing it to further their own ends. Do not let somebody's arbitrary "no" stop you. Find a way to turn the "no" into a "yes," or find a creative way to sidestep the "no." Do not let anybody stop you!

11. *You have an important decision to make and you do not know what to do. Which statement best describes your decision-making process?*

I really believe that if you are good and if you are smart and if you know your business, you have to go with your gut on occasion and go against the tide. In some of the best deals I have made, I went against what everybody else believed. Television producer Mark Burnett went from selling T-shirts on Venice Beach to reaching the pinnacle of Hollywood power because he followed his instincts about the kind of reality TV that would appeal to the masses. We all have instincts. The important thing is to know how to use them. You may have superb academic credentials, but if you do not use your instincts, you might have a hard time getting to and staying at the top.

12. *What is your attitude toward people?*

The world is a vicious and brutal place. We think we're civilized. In truth, it's a cruel world and people are ruthless. They act nice to your face, but underneath they're out to kill you. You have to know how to defend yourself. People will be mean and nasty and try to hurt you just for sport. Lions in the jungle only kill for food, but humans kill for fun. Even your friends are out to get you: they want your job, they want your house, they want your money, they want your wife, and they even want your dog. Those are your friends; your enemies are even worse! My motto is "Hire the best people, and don't trust them."

13. *When someone intentionally harms you or your reputation, how do you react?*

When someone crosses you, my advice is "Get even!" That is not typical advice, but it is real-life advice. If you do not get even, you are just a schmuck! When people wrong you, go after those people, because it is a good feeling and because other people will see you doing it. I love getting even. I get screwed all the time. I go after people, and you know what? People do not play around with me as much as they do with others. They know that if they do, they are in for a big fight. Always get even. Go after people that go after you. Don't let people push you around. Always fight back and always get even. It's a jungle out there, filled with bullies of all kinds who will try to push you around. If you're afraid to fight back people will think of you as a loser, a "schmuck"! They will know they can get away with insulting you, disrespecting you, and taking advantage of you. Don't let it happen! Always fight back and get even. People will respect you for it.

14. *You are "on a roll" and everything seems to be going your way. What do you do now?*

If you are on a quest for the golden ring, you cannot afford to be complacent. You can never rest, no matter how good things are going. Your current "good times" are only a result of the hard work and dedication you have put forth. What you do today will produce results tomorrow. If you want to keep the good times rolling, you have to keep on planting those seeds every day! If you stop focusing even for one minute, you will start slipping backwards.

It is true that a few people are born to be successful. They possess a special talent that makes it easy to succeed—the gifted musician, the natural athlete, or the talented businessperson. The vast majority of successful people were not handed success on a silver platter. They worked hard for it. They set goals, and they stayed focused until they reached them.

Some people are born with an exceptional talent that makes it easy for them to excel, like Mozart or Shakespeare. Most great successes weren't born that way. It took many years of hard work and intense focus to get to the top.

15. *What is your attitude toward the business of being married?*

Now, I have seen bad deals, I have seen bad partnerships, I have seen many business deals in litigation—and litigation is not nice—but there is nothing worse than a man and a woman who fight, especially when they are fighting over their assets, their business, their home, their cars, and everything else. It is terrible. You were in love with somebody, and now you are no longer in love. The hatred is so intense, far more intense than it usually gets in a business transaction. There is nothing more vicious than a man or woman going through a divorce. It is pure hell, like nothing else I have ever seen. You need a prenuptial agreement to protect yourself and your business interests.

Marriage is a contract unlike any other contract in life. You marry for love. But your signature on the marriage certificate is all about rights, duties, and property. It's a legally binding contract that knows nothing of love.

If the love dies, all you have left is a resentful ex-spouse and the marriage certificate. There's nothing more terrible than an ex-spouse with a ten-ton axe to grind, and no agreement on how your common property is to be divided. It usually leads to all-out war that is more vicious than any legal battle in business and could easily lead to your financial and emotional ruin. Always get a prenup. It's just too risky not to.

So how did you score on the test? Let's cut to the chase. If you scored a 46–60, you are making the grade! You are one of the top 2 percent who have what it takes to make it big. If you work hard, you may become more successful than someone with a high IQ or an MBA. I have seen it all my life. I went to the Wharton School of Finance with some great students. I still know many of them today and, with a few exceptions, they are not very successful. I have seen people who could not even get into Wharton, who went to other colleges or no college at all, but they focused on their goals and never quit. They worked hard and they loved what they were doing. So they ended up being more successful than the genius students at Wharton.

Hard work is my personal method for financial success. I know a lot of people who do not have great talent, but they are rich. You can do it, too. The principles in this book will help anyone no matter what their background. If you did not score between 46 and 60, then read this book now, underline what is missing in your life, and, especially important, absorb the attitudes expressed in my stories. Feel what I am feeling, and make my attitude your attitude. Then retake the test. You will score much higher after reading this book!

ZANKER'S TAKE

As President and Founder of The Learning Annex, I have had the opportunity to observe hundreds of supersuccessful people firsthand, millionaires and billionaires who have risen above the ordinary to achieve amazing things in life. They all possess one very important quality: persistence. Look at Donald Trump, for example; he personifies the word *persistence*. He never quit, even when he was down and out.

More than anything else, it takes persistence to do the things you need to do to get to the top. How many days do you feel like you can't do it anymore? Can't make the call or knock on the door. How many times can you get rejected, yet you know you are just so close? How many times do you have to ignore people hounding you for money, while you are moving heaven and earth to make you and your family's dreams happen? We have all been there. It is hard, but the rewards are great, so we don't stop until we achieve our dreams.

It takes persistence to knock on door after door and deal with rejection after rejection, without knowing whether you will ever be successful. And when you finally break through and land a great client or a great job or venture capital for your start-up business, it takes persistence to sign on the dotted line and commit to fulfilling what you promised you would do. It takes persistence to face the difficult problems that nobody can help you solve. It takes persistence to endure setbacks and come back with the same level of intensity and enthusiasm you had before. And when you finally succeed, it takes persistence to fight back when rivals, competitors, and bullies come after you to take you down.

I learned how persistence works long ago, when I was building The Learning Annex in the early 1980s. I wanted the owner of the famous New York food store Zabar's, Murray Klein, to speak on "How to Create a Great Food Market." I thought New Yorkers who love food—and there are plenty of them—would flock to this class. Zabar's was (and still is) a great New York food institution on the Upper West Side. I called and went to see Murray Klein, and in a very New York way he dismissed me and my request while he was busy yelling at the fish cutter to make the slices thinner. (If you've never been to Zabar's, you've got to go visit this place.) Murray Klein is a quintessential New Yorker.

Walking home, feeling rejected, I got an idea. The next morning, I called a florist, and told them to deliver $200 worth of flowers every day to Zabar's, with a note to Murray Klein saying, "Please teach at The Learning Annex." Remember this was the 1980s, and $200 bought a lot of flowers. I told the florist, "Keep delivering the flowers every day until I tell you to stop." By day nine, I started panicking that I was down $1,800 already, with not a word from Murray Klein.

Then the call came. "Zanker," Murray said, "What's it going to take for you to stop sending me those damn flowers? There's no room in my office anymore."

I said, "Give New Yorkers one night of your time."

Murray said, "I love your chutzpah. I'll do it."

And Murray surprised everyone and brought a spread of food to the class that was glorious. People ate for free all of Zabar's delicacies while Murray talked. He was brilliant bringing the food to class because everyone talked about it the next day. What great publicity for Zabar's. And the next day I got flowers from Murray with a card saying, "Zanker, that was fun, but I will never ever do it again!"

I've used this trick numerous times since then, and in fact more recently I got Jim Cramer from *Mad Money* the same way.

Let me tell you another story about persistence. When I bought back The Learning Annex in 2001, I wanted Robert Kiyosaki of *Rich Dad* fame to speak. I kept calling up his office, and he and his partner Sharon Lechter wouldn't take my calls. I read that he was speaking in Phoenix, so I left my home in Westchester County, New York at 5:00 A.M., and got on a plane at John F. Kennedy Airport to get to Phoenix. I got to the event on time, and I asked to meet with Robert during lunch. His assistant said, "I can't do it. You need an appointment."

I said, "I can't get an appointment; he's not returning my calls."

She said, "I'm sorry."

Taking a taxi back to the Phoenix Airport, I was very angry. How stupid. But on the flight back to New York, I decided I wouldn't quit.

So every day, at around 11:00 A.M., I'd call Robert and Sharon, and leave messages. It became a ritual. Like brushing your teeth in the morning, I would call Robert and Sharon every morning at about 11:00. I did this for about three months straight, never missing a day, and finally Sharon Lechter called me up. She said, "I'll be in New York next week, would you like to have lunch?"

I said, "Great."

She asked, "Where do you want to meet?"

I'm a guy who eats lunch at my desk, but the first restaurant that came to my mind was The 21 Club, a posh New York restaurant.

She said, "Great, I'll see you there."

I got to the restaurant an hour before we were supposed to meet, and I went to the maître d'. I gave him twenty dollars, and asked him, "When I get here for lunch, can you ask me if I want my usual table?"

He took my $20, and said, "No."

I went into my pocket, took out five more twenties, and gave them to him. He said, "I'll see you at one o'clock."

I walked in at 1:00, exactly when Sharon walked in, and the maître d' hugged me—he was almost overdoing it—and he said, "Mr. Zanker, nice to see you." He ushered us to a great table. Sharon was duly impressed.

In the end, the lunch was a great success because it was over that lunch we agreed Robert would speak just once for The Learning Annex. "Rich Dad" Robert Kiyosaki had such a great experience that the "once" became many times. It took me six months, but I was persistent and always knew I would get Robert to teach for The Learning Annex because "No" was not an option.

I see it all the time. The most successful people I have learned from just never take no for an answer. They have all had to endure big challenges to get to where they are. They've had to overcome the odds that stop most people from making it big. To do this, they've had to develop the habit of persistence. You are going to learn a lot in this book, but as a small business owner never giving up is the most important attribute you can learn.

TO SUM IT UP

Winners in life have a special quality that I call the Trump IT quality, which sets them apart from 98 percent of the population. There is a formula you can follow to be a winner in life. But you must be brutally honest with yourself. Getting rich is tough, and people get hurt. You have to be as tough as nails and willing to kick ass if you want to win. Take the preceding litmus test to see if you have the right stuff. Learn about the areas of your life you need to kick up a notch. Read this book and absorb the tough-attitude stories. Then retake the test and you will score much higher.

KEY POINTS

▶ Dream big because what you dream is what you will do.

▶ If you want to make tons of money, do not be shy: set a big goal.

▶ Be lean and hungry, and at every level set even higher goals and challenges for yourself.

▶ Take action every day, and stay focused for the long haul.

▶ Soak up more and more knowledge, so that you always know what you are doing.

▶ Pride yourself on your ability to find creative solutions to tough problems.

▶ Be passionate about your work.

▶ Never take no for an answer.

▶ Learn to trust your gut.

▶ Hire the best people, and do not trust them.

▶ Get even with people who do you wrong.

▶ Never stop focusing on your objectives, even when things are good.

▶ Always get a prenuptial agreement.

2

PASSION, PASSION, PASSION!

You have to love what you do or you are never going to be successful no matter what you do in life. If you love what you do, you are going to work harder, you are going to try harder, you are going to be better at it, and you're going to enjoy your life more. The most important things are knowing your business and loving what you do, both of which solve a lot of problems.

The first paragraph in my first book *The Art of the Deal* is: "I don't do it for the money. I've got enough, much more than I'll ever need. I do it to do it. Deals are my art form. Other people paint beautifully on canvas or write beautiful poetry. I like making deals, preferably big deals. That's how I get my kicks." Now it's 20 years later and I'm still making deals, big deals. That's *still* how I get my kicks.

It works. I focused on my passion, and a lot of money has come to me. I am much wealthier than I was when I wrote my first book. I am so passionate about my work that to me there is nothing better, which is the greatest feeling. Some nights I can't even sleep. I want to wake up so badly and go to work.

Since I wrote that book, I have gone through some really rough times. I almost lost everything in the early 90s, but I got through it all and survived and thrived. My real estate business is better than ever and fate has brought me some unexpected surprises. I have gotten into television with my hit show *The Apprentice,* and I own *Miss Universe* and *Miss USA,* two very successful beauty pageants broadcast on NBC. The Learning Annex speeches have also become a phenomenal hit. So here I am, with *The Apprentice* entering yet another season and The Learning Annex Wealth Expo touring the country.

My motivation for doing these projects was never the money. I wasn't even looking for these projects. But my reputation for being passionate about my work is well-known. What I do passionately every day fit well with these new enterprises, so they found me. You can't just sit around waiting for deals, opportunities, or a lucky break. You have to work passionately at something you love to do, and the momentum you build will work in your favor and bring other good things your way.

If money were my only goal, I would have passed up a lot of my most important work. For example, if I based my decision solely on monetary gain, I would have never done the Wollman Skating Rink in New York's Central Park. The rink, originally built in 1950, was closed by the city in 1980 for renovation. The city spent years and twenty million dollars on renovations, and in 1986 it was nowhere near finished. I love New York City, and I wanted to provide people with a wonderful recreational center in the heart of Manhattan. I had built major skyscrapers in less than two years. I felt I could easily renovate a skating rink in a matter of months. I took on the project to save the city time and money. My motive was to provide a service, not to make money.

FIND YOUR PASSION

Don't think about how you can make money. Instead think about what you can produce or what service you can offer that is valuable and useful to people and to your community. What needs to be improved? What can be done in a better or more efficient way? What problem can you solve? What needs can you fulfill? And most important, what will you have fun doing?

Sure, you need to get paid for your work, and you will if you provide something valuable. In the game of life, money is how you score. Yet the real fun is not in simply scoring; rather it is in the excitement you will have coming up with creative ways to get the ball in the goal. Find your passion in doing something useful for people and the money will follow.

It may sound simple, but I have become a billionaire many times over by sticking with this simple philosophy. Many people believe that I started out with a lot of money from my father. The truth is that when I started out in business, I was practically broke. My father didn't give me much money, but what he did give me was a good education and the simple formula for getting wealthy: work hard doing what you love.

In the early 70s, when New York City was in big financial trouble, the area around Grand Central Terminal on 42nd Street was quickly deteriorating. Many buildings were in foreclosure. The old Commodore Hotel, in terrible disrepair, was losing money by the fistful and becoming a hangout for derelicts. If someone hadn't done something soon, this area would've become a slum. I knew I could make money there, but I wanted to only if I could make a difference—only if I could take an ugly, run-down hotel and turn it into a beautiful and desirable place to stay. By transforming the Commodore into the new sleek Grand Hyatt, I created a renewal in that neighborhood that continues to this day and I made money doing it.

With everything you do, find a mission or grand purpose beyond money that you can become passionate about. Find the higher ground above the greedy exclusiveness of people who only care about money. Broaden your vision to see the total picture of what you are offering. Fill as many needs as you can: creating beauty, efficiency, health, security, and livelihood for as many people as possible.

If you want to do really big things in life, then you have to have monumental enthusiasm and passion. To be done right, every job requires passion. The doorman, the waiter, and the receptionist are there to greet each visitor with enthusiasm. No matter what your job is presently, do it with passion and magic will happen. You will meet the right person and get noticed. I have seen this over and over again. How much more passion is needed to be a great entrepreneur or artist? Find a noble cause and get behind it with all your heart and soul.

Without passion, life lacks luster. Passion gives you the intestinal fortitude you need to never give up. My Grand Hyatt triumph did not come without the high price of dedication, persistence, and hard work. Through all the challenges, my passion for turning something ugly into something compelling and appealing kept me going and enabled me to get many other people to share in my vision.

How do you find your passion? Try this: For a moment, put aside any judgments and rational assessment you may have. Start daydreaming about what you really and truly love to do. If you could do one thing in life, what would it be? What do you get so caught up in the fun of doing that you lose track of time? What would you enjoy doing so much you would do it even without getting paid? What have you been doing when you were very satisfied with yourself? What kinds of things put you in a "zone" and lead to peak experiences? If you could be somebody that you admire, who would it be?

Then be realistic. Doing what you love also means doing something you can do, something you are good at. Think about your strengths. Find out what you are good at. Think about your unique talents and the things you have done that you are most proud of. What kinds of activities come easily and naturally to you? When you think of work you love, think big! Think of amazing accomplishments. Think of the joy and fulfillment you will derive from your work. When you do work that you love, it is no longer work because the activity itself is a source of energy. Steve Jobs, cofounder of Apple and Pixar, is passionate about computer technology. He was not the best computer designer, but he was the most passionate. Jobs' passion has made him one of the most prolific innovators of our generation.

BE A DOER NOT A DREAMER

Passion is more important than brains or talent. I have seen some really talented, brainy people fail because of lack of passion. They are what I call "idea people." You have probably seen them, too. They always seem to have great new ideas they are thinking about doing someday—but they never do anything about them.

The ideas always stay in their heads and never get in their hearts. Without heart the ideas fizzle out fast. Ideas themselves are light and fluffy. They need tremendous passion to make them into concrete, stone, and glass. You have to bring your ideas down to earth. Take your ideas and add the weight of passion to them as soon as possible before they disappear into thin air. Passion is the magic ingredient that zaps you with the fierce drive for completion of every endeavor. I have seen less-talented people propel themselves to great success on high-octane passion. You must have it to compete and thrive in this world.

You know, I learned about passion from my father. People ask, "Did you learn construction from your father?" The answer is yes, I learned all about construction from my father. You know what I really learned from him? My father worked on Saturdays, on Sundays, seven days a week. He loved working. He was a happy guy. When he would go to a job, he would actually go around to see if apartments had been swept and cleaned. He had an expression he called "mint condition"—the apartments have to be in mint condition. So he would go around on Saturdays and Sundays, and he loved it. Building in Brooklyn and Queens, every penny mattered.

He would build an apartment house, while across the street

someone else would also be building an apartment house. My father would get it done faster and cheaper, and it would be nicer. The other guy would go out of business, and my father would buy that apartment house and fix it up. I learned from my father that work can make you happy.

I got my passion for work from my father. I'm so passionate about my work that I only sleep three to four hours every night. I can't wait to get up in the morning and go to work because I love my work so much. If you love what you are doing, you are probably not going to sleep more than three or four hours. When you are waking up to something you love, it is hard to sleep more than that.

For example, one of my greatest passions is making deals. I love to make the big score and to make the big deal. I love to crush the other side and take the benefits. Why? Because there is nothing greater. For me it is even better than sex, and I love sex. But when you hit, when the deals are going your way, it is the greatest feeling! You hear lots of people say that a great deal is when both sides win. That is a bunch of crap. In a great deal you win—not the other side. You crush the opponent and come away with something better for yourself. In negotiations I love to go for the complete win. That is why I have made so many good deals.

My other great passion, creating beautiful real estate developments, has been a major reason for my success. The world of construction and real estate development is known for being demanding and difficult. It requires great precision. Construction can't be haphazard because people can be injured. Happenstance is not acceptable. I love the challenge of having to be precise and do a meticulous job. Because I love it, I am very good at it. I have applied that approach to everything I do.

I remember we had a new employee at the Trump Organization who could not understand why we spent time doing property checks to the extent that we did. We were already established and the buildings were well-known and highly praised, but we would still do checks. Sometimes, I would personally visit the property just to give it a walk-through. What the employee didn't understand is that it is something we do to make sure our standards are being maintained, and we do it often to stay on top of things. It may not be necessary, but it is something we consider to be important.

I love to take an undeveloped piece of property and turn it into something magnificent. Beauty and elegance, whether in a woman or a work of art, are other passions of mine. Beauty is not something superficial, not just something pretty to look at. It is a product of style, and it comes from deep inside. For me, my passion for style and my success are completely interwoven. I would not want to have one without the other.

When I head up to my office in Trump Tower in New York City, I enjoy looking at the magnificent atrium I created. I love to see the crowds of people oohing and aahing at the stunning marble and the breathtaking 80-foot waterfall. I love to see the emotional response, the thrill and the appreciation of the extraordinary beauty of it all. I resonate with them. I'm a little closer to them even though we've never met, because that is the same feeling I had when I built Trump Tower.

In truth I am dazzled as much by my own creations as are the tourists and glamour hounds that flock to Trump Tower, The Trump Taj Mahal in Atlantic City, 40 Wall Street or any of my other properties. I know people are responding to my passion for beauty and style, which is reflected in my work. Style moves people, and the most successful people have style in spades. Creating extraordinarily beautiful buildings really excites me and drives me to overcome the greatest obstacles.

Vince McMahon, chairman of World Wrestling Entertainment, is worth a billion dollars. Vince McMahon not only loves what he does but he is also really good at it. When I did a job in Portland, Oregon, I went to see McMahon in action. I was amazed. I was at his regular venue in Portland and the fight was being staged in front of 30,000 people. It was totally sold out. I said, "Vince, is this place sold out?" He said it sold out a year ago. I said, "What about WrestleMania in Detroit, is it sold out?" He said it was sold out five hours after he put the tickets on sale. There were 82,000 people in Ford Field football stadium in Detroit to see the show. I said, "You are really good at this." He had to manage hundreds of technicians and many details and people. Vince was right on top of everything, and I said to myself, here is a guy who really is special. He loves what he does, and he really understands his subject. That is why he is so good at it and so successful.

Now, if you know the truth, you know the Turner folks tried to take over the WWE in the late 90s and it was a disaster. They could not beat McMahon at his own game because he knew it so well. When I talk about success I always start off with one topic and the rest sort of flows, and the topic is: you have to love what you do. Vince McMahon and many other people I know are successful because they love what they do. If you love your work, you are going to work harder, and everything is going to come easier. To be successful, even if it's a job, you need to love what you do.

I have a friend who was born into a ruthless family. His father is a vicious, miserable, horrible human being, but other than that, he's a very nice guy (kidding!). The father is a Wall Street legend, a very tough guy, and he makes lots of money. If I mentioned his name, you would all know him. His son, let's call him Stan, is just a nice person. I am friendly with both of them, and it is easy for me to like the son, but the father is just too much.

Stan was working on Wall Street with his father, and he was miserable. One time Stan's wife called me and said, "Oh, Donald, he's miserable, he's unhappy, it's just not working. My marriage is no good, nothing is good." I said, "Why are you telling me this? I can't do anything about it." Stan was failing on Wall Street, he hated it, but he could not do anything about it because he did not want to disappoint his father.

Stan is a member of a very prestigious golf club in Westchester. One day he was put in charge of a beautiful and expensive golf course renovation project, not because they believed he would do a good job but just because they liked him.

As it turned out, he was unbelievable. He was at the course every day at five in the morning. The project took six months instead of a year to finish, and it came out ten times better than anyone expected and for less money. I said to him, "Stan, you are unbelievable." His wife called and said, "He's great, and he changed so much." Everybody was happy, his kids, his wife, everybody. He was incredible, he kicked the contractor's ass, and he watched him like a hawk. After Stan finished the course, they gave him an award and had a dinner in his honor. Stan was a big hero.

After that, Stan went back to Wall Street, and he started to fail. When he told me he was failing I said, "Stan, you are doing the wrong thing." He said, "I can't help it, I have to do it for my father." I said, "You are doing the wrong thing. You've got to go into construction, renovation, or golf course building. You've got to do it. You'll be great at it, you'll do well." He said, "I can't do it."

He became totally miserable. Then finally about three years ago, he got wise and quit his Wall Street job to go into construction. Now he is doing phenomenally well because he loves his job. He is not making the same money he would have made if he were a Wall Street killer, but he is happy and he loves what he does and he loves getting up in the morning. He now sees himself as a winner. When I see him now, he is always beaming and looking healthy. He has a new lease on life and has become a different person because he had the guts to go against tradition, take control of his life, and change.

So, if your life is not what you want it to be, don't be afraid to ask yourself whether you are doing what you want and what is right for you. No matter how old you are measure yourself against your own feelings, ambitions, and goals, not those of others. That might mean standing up to friends, family, and colleagues who think they know what is best for you. Plug in to your own electricity. It might flow better through another socket.

GRACE UNDER PRESSURE

Another key to your success will be how well you deal with pressure. If you want to be successful at anything in life, you have to be able to handle pressure. Whether you are buying or building real estate, starting your own company, or climbing your way up the corporate ladder, you need to deal with a large amount of pressure. Successful Wall Street wheeler-dealers, doctors, lawyers, athletes, politicians, and entertainers live a life filled with pressure. How do they do it? How do they live happy and successful lives when there is so much pressure?

A lot of times, stress has more to do with focusing on what you love than with anything else. I have learned that it is important to focus on the solution, not the problem. If you put all your energy into the problem, how much passion do you have left for finding a solution? I have known developers who get caught up in lengthy discussions with everybody involved when they encounter something unexpected such as zoning restrictions, code violations, too much groundwater, or missing materials. They spend too much time discussing what caused the problem and who is to blame. Then they start imagining the worst: the job will be late, they will be way over budget, the banks will pull the financing, or the city will pull the permits. That energy would be better spent on finding a solution.

When I started my career in real estate, I had a problem. I had no money to invest in the properties I wanted. But I didn't focus on it and let it stop me. I focused all my attention on buying properties without money!

My advice is to acknowledge the problem and then move on to a more positive level. If we were to say to ourselves, "I'm so unfocused" instead of "I'm so stressed out," I think we could clear things up more quickly. The more focused I am on doing things I love, the less stress I experience.

But the fact is, not everybody is cut out to be successful. I want to tell you about the negatives of business as well as the positives. I want to talk about the fact that most people are not cut out to deal with the high stress level of being a great success. I don't know why, but some people are just not able to do it.

I have seen so many people who are geniuses: they have high IQs, they had all A's in college, they had all A's in high school, they have gone to the best schools—Harvard, Wharton—but they can't handle pressure. I have gotten to a point where I know a lot of smart people, but I do not know a lot of people who can handle pressure.

One of the things I love about sports is you see in a very small period of time whether an athlete folds or thrives under pressure. Most of them fold. But there are some great athletes that do better under pressure. Look at Tiger Woods, Derek Jeter, or Tom Brady, they all seem to thrive under pressure. In sports you can find this out quickly; whereas in the business world it may take ten or fifteen years to know whether you can handle pressure. I think it is vital that you know whether you can withstand pressure. If you can't, there is nothing wrong with that. It is great to have a job you like, get married, raise some kids, and live a happy life. That in itself is a form of success and is a good thing, though it wouldn't be for me.

I have had friends, many friends, who went to the Wharton School with me who were very smart. By the way, I was actually a good student. Believe it or not, I was very good at math and science. A lot of people find it hard to believe I was a good student because they don't see that part of my personality. They think I am smart, but they do not see how I could sit down and study. But I did!

I have had some very smart friends who I have kept in touch with. One person in particular was a total genius and he never made it. He has a nice job working for an accounting firm, but he went out recently to buy a house and he was a basket case. He called me and asked, "Do you think I'm making a mistake? I don't know what I'm doing. I'm so nervous. I'm buying a house. I mean, what do I do? Do I borrow?" He was devastated over the fact that he was buying a house. After he bought the house, this brilliant guy called me and said, "Donald, I bought a house. Do you think I did the right thing? I have a mortgage. Oh, my God, will it be all right?" Here is a guy with a 180 IQ, and he cannot sleep and he cannot have sex with his wife because he is so stressed. I said, "What's the purpose of buying a house if you can't sleep with your wife? What kind of a house is this?"

He is a guy who advises people about how to make money. He is a very successful accounting-type person and a total genius, but when it comes to spending his own money, he is a basket case. After about ten calls from him, I told him, "Jim, you are so lucky you have a good job, because you could never, ever work for yourself." He was insulted. It is true, but he was insulted nonetheless. I said, "You couldn't do it because you can't handle the pressure."

I have been through a lot. I have had great success. I have also had some really tough times, like when the real estate market collapsed in the early 90s. I owed many billions of dollars, and the banks were after my ass. It was not exactly fun! I had every major bank after me. Everybody in my industry was in big trouble. I had some friends and some enemies in the business who I thought were really tough guys, but most of them could not handle the bad times like they handled the good times. Most of them went out of business. All my friends were going bankrupt. I was very close, but I never went bankrupt. Even though it was not much fun and I never want to go through it again, in some ways it wasn't so bad. I slept very well, and I managed to keep my faculties. It is not that I trained for it; I didn't train for it. But that awful experience taught me that I can handle pressure. Most people crawled into a corner, put their fingers in their mouths, and said, "Mommy, Mommy, take me home!"

I learned that I can handle pressure. I did not back down under pressure. I turned it back on the banks and let them accept some of the blame. I figured it was the bank's problem, not mine. What the hell did I care? I actually told one bank, "I told you you shouldn't have loaned me that money. I told you that goddamn deal was no good. You knew you were charging me too much interest." I was just kidding—but maybe not. That is what I had to say. It was not great, but it was better than dropping to my knees like other people did. Banks are afraid of getting sued. That is why I say there are ways of getting through problems. You have to love what you do, and you have to be able to deal with pressure.

Yes, I never went bankrupt, but I was in deep, deep trouble. Fortunately, I had great relationships with banks. In the 1980s I treated my banks well and so, in the 1990s they did not want to hurt me. They wanted to kill me in some ways, because that is what banks do when you do not pay them, but they did not want to do to me what they did to many other people.

There is an old saying: "Be careful who you step on going up because you meet the same people coming down." It is true. I knew a man in the real estate business whose name I will not mention. He was a pretty well-known guy. He was a very arrogant guy. He built buildings like I did and he always looked down on the bankers. He treated them very, very badly. Sometimes he would talk to their wives at dinners and say, "I can't believe your husband's a banker. Look at all the money I'm making, and he's not." He would intentionally make them feel bad.

I had the opposite approach to bankers. I would say, "You're the greatest!" Even if I was making a fortune and they weren't, I would say, "You're the greatest!" Why hurt these people? The man went on like that for six or seven years. He borrowed a lot of money, and he built a lot of buildings. When the real estate market crashed, the banks came down hard on him, much harder than they came down on me. They came down really hard on him because he was an arrogant asshole. One of the bankers told me that this arrogant, tough, mean, nasty guy dropped to his knees, begged them not to foreclose on personal guarantees, and cried like a baby. He cried—on his knees! So you know what they did? They put him right out of business. I have not heard from that guy since.

DO WHAT FEELS GOOD

In the early 90s I was in a ton of debt. I had gone from the smartest guy in town to a complete zero. One night I went into the conference room where my accountants were still working, and the mood was definitely stressful because everyone was focused on unpleasant things. I decided we needed to change the focus to things that were fun. So I started describing to everyone all of my plans for future projects and developments and how fantastic they were going to be. I went into detail about them, painting a vivid picture of success. My accountants all acknowledged later that they thought I had actually flipped out. But from that moment on, our focus changed from looking at our big problem to looking at our terrific future.

Things changed for the better. Changing the focus to what we loved doing was the turning point. After that I actually started negotiating new deals, even though I was in no position to do them, because it made me feel good. Sure, I owed a lot of money, but my mind-set was very positive. Now my company is more successful and productive than ever.

Another way I deal with business pressure is to realize how fragile life is. I lost my top three executives in a helicopter crash in Atlantic City. When something like that happens you realize how delicate life is. I have a great estate in Florida called The

Mar-a-Lago Club, and, when I can, I allow returning Iraqi war veterans that are wounded to come to Mar-a-Lago and use my private beach and oceanfront. I have even been told by my staff that the most beautiful people they have ever seen were those coming back from Iraq without arms and without legs and I am glad I could welcome them home at Mar-a-Lago.

I am a businessman. I find that a lot of businesspeople are streetwise, and people who are streetwise know that business really doesn't matter. It is just a game, and we are all here to have a good time while we can. People ask me, "How do you handle pressure? How do you make billion-dollar deals and finance them with enormous bank loans? How can you sleep at night? How do you go on television in front of millions of people?"

The truth is, it does not matter. What the hell difference does it make? You see what is going on in Iraq; you have seen a tsunami wipe out hundreds of thousands of people. Think about how 3,000 people died in the World Trade Center on September 11, 2001—tragic; and how 300,000 people died from the tsunami in Asia in 2004; 100 times more. What does it really matter if you have a big presentation to give to the president of Citibank at 9 A.M.? Just be wise and have a great sense of humor because problems that may seem big to you really do not matter in the grand scheme of things.

You know, all of my life, people have told me about bad stuff that could possibly happen. They talk to me about market crashes, wars, diseases, earthquakes, and tsunamis. People say I should eat this food or that food so I will not get cancer. A lawyer friend of mine—a great guy, a very smart guy—came up to me the other day and said he heard that I had spoken in front of over 62,000 people in Los Angeles. He said, "How do you do that? Don't you get scared?" I said, "I don't want to think about it." It is true: I *don't* want to think about it. I just do it. Then he called me up the next day and said, "That's the smartest thing I've ever heard."

The truth is I don't think about anything except what I have to think about to do a great job. I will have plenty of time when I am an old man to think about other things; now I just think about how to get the job done.

LEARN FROM YOUR MISTAKES

Everyone has good times and bad times. Everyone makes good deals and bad deals. You just have to live with that. All great deal-makers, who make hundreds of deals, have made bad deals. No matter what you do to avoid it, sometimes deals just do not work out. Rather than get depressed and down on myself, I live by a little formula I call the Formula of Knowledge. Using this formula, I learn not only from the good times but also from the bad times.

THE FORMULA OF KNOWLEDGE

The best way to learn is through studying the history of successes and failures in your industry.

The Formula of Knowledge is the best way to learn because learning from someone else's mistakes is faster and easier than making them yourself. For example, you don't have to go through an early 1990s real estate crash like I did to know what to do in that situation. Because of the way things go in life, lots of times life forces you to learn from your own mistakes, but it is much better if you can learn from others' mistakes rather than your own.

NEVER GIVE UP

Another thing: if you want to be successful, you can never, ever quit. You can never, ever give up. Now, if you love what you do, you are not going to give up, because you love it. Sometimes you will feel like giving up. It may seem impossible to try again. But that is the most important time, because it is the time when you begin to learn important information about what you are doing—information you need to succeed.

You have to be patient as well as enthusiastic when it comes to your goals. Think big, but be realistic. I have waited thirty years for some things to happen. Look at media mogul Rupert Murdoch: he waited many years to buy *The Wall Street Journal*. He always wanted it and he knew he would get it. Rupert is a true genius. You will always encounter obstacles; in fact, it is a good idea to count on them. See them as a challenge instead of an obstacle and you will find that you have the ability to move beyond them. It is most important to be tenacious—do not ever give up. Just keep moving forward, keep your goals clear, and don't give in to discouragement or setbacks.

I can tell you many stories about friends of mine who are really, really smart and amazing—the smartest people you can imagine—and yet they never made it, because they quit. I can also tell you stories about friends of mine who were not as smart. If you gave them aptitude tests, they would score 25 percent lower. They are now some of the richest guys in the world, because they had something different; they didn't quit. If you love something, if you really love it, you are less inclined to quit.

Part of the problem is that we want to avoid painful situations like not getting a loan, losing a deal or a customer you have been after, or even losing your business or your wife. As I said before, you can't let this stuff hold you back. Do not think about the pain and just keep going, like the great athletes do.

I could not believe my ears when I heard Michelle Sorro, a candidate on *The Apprentice* Los Angeles, tell me she was going to throw in the towel and quit rather than face me in the boardroom. I couldn't believe it because I am used to dealing with the toughest people in business, who would never dream of quitting.

Michelle was having a rough time as project manager. Her teammates did not like her and were giving her a hard time. She ended up leading her team to a stunning defeat. Yet instead of toughing it out, she quit. I was amazed that anyone would so easily throw away an opportunity to compete for a high-powered position. We have over 50,000 people waiting in line to audition for *The Apprentice*. She had been chosen, and yet she just threw it all away without a fight.

You do not get many lucky breaks like that in life. There is one thing that I teach over and over again: if you want to be successful in business and in life, never, ever give up. Never quit. You can never be successful if you give up.

Michelle rationalized away her lack of grit with a barrage of excuses built around the idea that her experience on *The Apprentice* was not what she had expected or signed on for. She never imagined she would have to live outdoors in a tent in the rain. I said to Michelle, "That's life. Every day people face a lot worse in life. Life is not always going to turn out the way you expect."

Every day is a new adventure. There are no guarantees. You can never know what is going to come at you, and sometimes it is pretty horrible. You have to be strong to survive, and you can never give in without a fight. Quitters do not stand a chance.

Michelle's quitting made me wonder if young people today lack the backbone to keep going. I read a new study which found that today's college students are, in fact, more narcissistic and self-centered than ever before.

The psychologists who conducted the study speculated that the behaviors of the students are a direct result of the way they were raised by their parents and taught in the school system. Since birth, many of these youngsters were fed a steady stream of compliments on how wonderful and special they were. The "self-esteem movement" of the 80s and 90s became a national fad and all the parents were doing it.

Too many hollow compliments are not healthy for kids. It is okay to let your children know they are special. It is a part of being a loving parent, but do not overdo it. To constantly lavish praise on your children for every little thing they do is too much. Do not be too easy on them. Let your children work hard to gain your praise. They will value it more.

I always taught my kids that they needed to work hard for everything they got in life and that all the luxuries they enjoy were because of my hard work. I taught them that if they want to share in the rewards, they have to share the work. Donald Jr., Ivanka, and Eric now work with me at The Trump Organization. They are working on deals, and I am teaching them everything I know about real estate. They were all excellent students and are doing a great job for me. I was blessed with great children to start with, but they seem to have a great natural talent.

If you overcompliment a child, you give him or her an inflated sense of self-worth, and they start to believe they are entitled to success in life without even trying. But it is not true. When they grow up they will find out that the world is much more difficult than you led them to believe. Then, if they cannot get something right away, they quit. Quitting is a habit that is hard to break.

My daughter Ivanka was asked to be in an MTV documentary called *Born Rich*. The show included Georgina Bloomberg, Luke Weil, Cody Franchetti, Si Newhouse IV, Josiah Hornblower, and Ivanka, among others. Some of these kids did nothing to dispel the stereotype of the spoiled rich kid. Some of them took for granted the wealth that had been laid at their feet and spoke disrespectfully about their parents. I could not believe it! Fortunately, Ivanka was different. She was poised, intelligent, and respectful when talking about her life and family, and was grateful for the advantages she had been given. I was very proud of Ivanka.

In real life there are some things that you just cannot do. People who tell their children that they can do anything they want are being unrealistic; some things are just not possible. Yet you do not want to discourage them. The trick is to be a skeptical optimist and to pick your battles. When you think you can win, go full-steam ahead and never quit, but also realize your limitations.

People tell me that I would be a success at anything. However, that is not true. I am primarily a builder, and then got a little lucky on TV. I'm a TV personality. These are some of the things I can do, and I put an enormous amount of passion into doing them well, but there are many things I cannot do. I am not good at computers. I know that no matter how hard I tried I could never make it big with computers. I don't have the great love for the computer that the greatest information-age entrepreneurs have. They just don't interest me.

Life is full of challenges and obstacles that get in our way. It is not possible to take on every challenge in life. We can, however, pick out something that we are excited by and think we can do. Then, when we encounter problems, we can climb over, go around, or go under until we reach our goal. I do not let anyone in my organization give up on a project until every possibility of success has been explored. I bought the land for Trump Place on Riverside Drive in New York's Upper West Side way back in 1974, and it is finally reaching completion in 2008. I stuck with it for over thirty years. I never gave up.

GET OUT OF YOUR COMFORT ZONE

The readers of *BusinessWeek* magazine voted me "the world's most competitive business leader." I do not know whether that is true as I know many fierce competitors. I am honored all the same, because I pride myself on my competitiveness and my drive to transcend the ordinary. You have to constantly challenge yourself to achieve greater and greater accomplishments. To do that, you have to leave your comfort zone. I have become one of the biggest developers in New York. There is tremendous competition in New York, so I am always on my toes and always trying to do better. I also compete with myself. I keep challenging myself to move forward and to maintain my momentum. I always strive to do things better, no matter how much success I may have achieved. For example, the Trump brand is now one of the most recognizable and valuable trademarks. It is synonymous with the very best things in life. When I was looking for a brand of vodka to bear the Trump trademark, I wanted only the finest, superpremium vodka, and I wanted to deliver the product to consumers in the style worthy of the Trump trademark. I found that vodka. I did the same with the Trump line of shirts, ties, and suits sold at Macy's, and they are all doing very well. I push myself to deliver the very best in everything I do because it has my name on it.

Somebody once asked me why I am never satisfied with where I am in life. It is simple: that is not who I am. If I were satisfied, I would not be Donald Trump. I found out from experience that it doesn't work for me. If you rest on your laurels, you are through. In the late 80s I thought I had made it big and did not have to work hard anymore. I quickly learned that the world is a changing place. You cannot stand still. If you do, life will pass you by.

I like to live my life on the cutting edge of progress—not for the money but for the sheer joy of participation. I would never give that up. I have noticed that real estate people never retire. They just keep making deals and fixing up their properties even into their eighties and nineties. For some reason they never retire—must be their love for their work.

TAKE ACTION

It is good to dream big. You will get nowhere unless you create big dreams, but you must have the courage to make those dreams real. Once you set your goals, start looking for opportunities to start acting on them. If you hesitate when an opportunity presents itself to you, it may be the fear of failure that makes you procrastinate. Break through this fear, for if you make a habit of procrastinating then all your goals become empty promises that will never be fulfilled. Always keep your promises to yourself by making a habit of acting on your goals.

After you discover what you love doing, you have to take action. I started buying and selling property when I was still a student at the Wharton School of Finance. You should get involved with what you love doing quickly at whatever level you can. It should be and remain enjoyable for you. As an example, Katie Couric is not having fun—you can see it in her eyes. She just doesn't want to be on the evening news and it shows. Also study books and learn from experienced people in the field. Then, as soon as you can, start doing it. Do not wait around for the "right time" or until you are perfect. It will never happen. Start right away. You will learn more from doing than you would learn from anything else.

You have to get the knowledge, you have to get into a field

that you really like, and you have to go out there and kick ass. That is all you have to do. Get out there and go for it!

ZANKER'S TAKE

To do something really well you have to love it. But it is not easy. Most people grow up being taught that work is not fun. Parents and teachers want you to work hard in school. And the rest of the time you can have fun doing what you want. Playing dodgeball is fun, going to school is not fun. Then, as a young adult you have to pick a profession. Most of us are unprepared. We cannot imagine how work can be fun because we have been conditioned to think otherwise.

So we are lured into jobs that our parents favor; jobs that lead to an automatic paycheck and a high level of prestige. Whether we actually like the career is irrelevant and does not figure into the decision. Prestige and money are a dangerous seduction for a young person making a career decision. Many young people gravitate toward careers that will impress other people. Their decisions are fatally flawed by the fact that the people they are trying to impress are not really that discriminating.

My father was an immigrant from Poland who designed fashionable women's suits and coats in the New York City garment district. He seemed to always be quitting his job and going to work for another company. He always seemed happy in his work, but if he was so happy, then why was he always quitting? I didn't understand that as a kid. The answer is that he did what he loved. His love for being a garment designer empowered him to quit whenever his employer messed with his designs, substituted cheaper materials, or did something that offended his principles. His love of his work gave him the backbone to stand up for himself. An assembly line worker hates what he or she does and is nervous about unemployment—it seems crazy because if you hate your job, you shouldn't be so nervous about losing it. But if you are not doing what you love, you will never feel secure in your work. You'll live in fear of being "found out." But do what you love, and you'll have the "kick ass" attitude you need to succeed, even if it means changing jobs and staying out of the assembly line "comfort zone."

I have a doctor friend who decided in high school what he wanted to do. He wanted a quick route to money and prestige. He never considered whether he would like it. Now he regrets his choice, and he is always telling me how much he hates it. Everyone thinks that they want financial security. But, actually, the happiest people are those who love what they do. Knowing that work can be fun is a good start. And once you find out what you love, you are almost there.

When I was first starting out, I thought I wanted to be a filmmaker. But the studies were boring. So I started something that I thought I was doing just for the money, The Learning Annex. For a while I was operating under the pretext that I was a filmmaker running a temporary business to make ends meet. But I soon realized that what I really loved was learning. It would have been great if I could have been a student for the rest of my life because I really like to learn new things. Whenever I went into a bookstore I would be captivated by the self-help section, and would spend hours looking through all the titles. I brought in the self-help experts who authored those books to teach at The Learning Annex. I would be thrilled to learn from these people, and I knew customers would be thrilled, too.

I stuck with The Learning Annex because it was exciting, and running it became the greatest career I could have ever imagined. It is not work at all; it is so much fun! I get to learn all the time from the greatest teachers in the world. I find "gurus" I want to learn from, convince them to share their knowledge with my students (which includes me) and I am in bliss. That is not work . . . it's what I love. It is like discovering a good restaurant and sharing it with friends. Finding the great teachers of the world and sharing them with my students makes me happy. So I am good at it. And prestige is a funny thing. If you do anything well enough, it becomes prestigious. And I am making a pile of money. Do what you love and the money will follow. It has for me and I am positive it will for you.

There was a guy who used to work for me that was proficient at what he did, but he had no passion for it. It was just a job to pay his mortgage. I fired him. Everyone was shocked. "How could you do that, he was good at his job?" But I didn't want people in my organization who didn't have a passion for their jobs. I believe they can ruin a company. If you are going to work at The Learning Annex, you've got to have excitement in what our mission is. Work somewhere else if it is just going to be a job. This same guy wrote me a beautiful letter a few years later thanking me for firing him. After I fired him, he started traveling around the world, and started to write about his travels. He is now a well-known travel writer and has written several books. He even occasionally teaches a class at The Learning Annex about breaking into travel writing. He found his true passion and is successful at it.

TO SUM IT UP

Never do anything just for money. Do it for love. To be supersuccessful you have to love what you are doing. Find a career you are passionate about. You will need passion to overcome obstacles, recover from setbacks, and make it through the tough times. Sure, money is a scorecard, and it is certainly useful, but it should not be the be-all and end-all. Give your goals substance and assign them a value that is not monetary. To be a winner in life, find a passion, get out of your comfort zone, and be a doer. Learn to handle pressure, to bounce back from failure, and to never give up.

KEY POINTS

▶ Find your passion and love what you do.

▶ Do not do things you don't like just for the money.

▶ Do your best, be passionate, and good things will come to you.

▶ Give your goals values that are not monetary.

▶ Know that passion conquers fear.

▶ Serve your passion by taking action every day.

▶ Take great joy in doing a great job.

▶ Focus on the solution, not on the problem.

▶ Handle pressure by learning not to dwell on negative thoughts and opinions of others.

▶ Learn from mistakes, but do not let them take you down.

▶ Be mentally tough and never give up.

▶ Push yourself out of your comfort zone.

3

BASIC
INSTINCTS

really believe that if you are good and you are smart, you can go with your gut. You need to go against the tide. In some of the best deals I have made, I went against what everybody else believed. My actions were very counterintuitive.

For my first five years in business, I was buying and renovating houses in Brooklyn and Queens with my dad. I decided I wanted to get involved in Manhattan real estate development because, to me, Manhattan was the big time. My father, though he was very successful, never did anything in Manhattan. Everybody told me not to go to Manhattan; I would never make it there. I did not have any money, but I was starting to do well in Brooklyn and Queens. The problem was I did not know anybody in Manhattan.

In the summer of 1973 the Penn Central Railroad filed for bankruptcy. Among the assets were abandoned yards in the West 60s and the West 30s. I had seen Penn Central's 100 acres of undeveloped riverfront property in Manhattan many times and had always thought that it had a lot of potential. At that time a lot of neighborhoods on the West Side were considered dangerous places to live because of drug dealers and welfare hotels. However, I could see how that could easily be changed. There were magnificent old brownstones on West 84th Street, just a few blocks from Central Park. I was convinced that it was only a matter of time before other people discovered the property's value.

People said I would never be able to pull it off and develop the land. Nobody in his or her right mind was interested in that property. The city was in trouble, and things were bad for developers. Among other problems, very few permits were being issued for new buildings. I pressed on anyway, because I felt in my gut that this was going to be big—and after all, what did I have to lose by trying? I met with the man in charge of selling off the assets of the railroad. I sold him on the deal. I worked on getting zoning approvals, fought the community board, and went before the City Planning Commission and the Board of Estimate.

The rest is history. In the meantime, I had started renovating the Commodore Hotel into the Grand Hyatt. These two projects gave me a much needed track record. On July 29, 1974, I acquired options to purchase the two waterfront properties from the Penn Central Railroad—West 59th Street to West 72nd Street and West 34th Street to West 39th Street—for $62 million with no money down. All because I went with my gut and did not quit.

Another deal was 40 Wall Street, which for a period of about a year before the Chrysler Building and the Empire State Building were built in 1931, was the tallest building in the world. Then it was the tallest building in downtown Manhattan until the World Trade Center was completed in 1972. I am sad to say since the World Trade Center went down, the seventy-two-story 40 Wall Street building is again the tallest building in downtown Manhattan.

It was 1993 and the market was horrible. I was not exactly doing great financially. I should not have been buying anything, because I was in trouble, but I bought the building at 40 Wall Street for $1 million. I just recently turned down a $535 million offer for it. That is pretty amazing. I took a risk, and it was not easy. Frankly, putting up $1 million in those days was very hard for me. I still had to carry the costs of the building. I still had to fix the building. That was a lot of money.

Times were bad—believe it or not I had a hard time coming up with $1 million to buy the building. That is sad. If you can't get together $1 million to buy a building, you have some pretty big problems. I was hard up. I went to four or five of the smartest real estate guys in New York, and I asked them to come in as partners with me on the deal. They would not touch it. They said it was a loser. I also had major real estate firms turn me down. I said, "Let's go fifty-fifty. I'll put up half a million dollars." It was peanuts to them, but they all turned me down. One guy said, "It's a money pit."

It was a money pit; I made a lot of money with it. Two of the real estate guys I tried to partner with told me it was the worst deal they *never* made. If they had had the instincts to go against the tide and put up half a million bucks, they would have made $270 million or even more! The one person who loved the deal was a brilliant real estate man named Jerry Speyer of Tishman-Speyer—nobody else.

In spite of what everybody said, I was really sold on 40 Wall Street. It was a seventy-two-story building, a total of 1.3 million square feet. I could break even if I only rented out the retail store on Wall Street. How could I lose? However, there was a dark mood around properties in downtown Manhattan, and few could see the value of the building. So I went with my gut and put up the $1 million myself and the risk paid off. I like to go against the tide. I feel it is important to go against the tide, to go with your gut—if you think you have that talent.

In reality it was an even better deal than that; I actually got this property for nothing. I challenged the real estate tax assessment on the property and was able to get a $4 million tax reduction. I settled with the city for more money than I had paid for the building. Then I got money back from tax refunds, so I bought the building for less than nothing—and today it makes a fortune. It went from 100 percent empty to 100 percent full very quickly.

You have to know what you are doing. You have to have confidence in yourself and confidence to know that what you are doing is right. You will have your biggest successes when you go against the tide. Many people get consultants and pay them a lot of money. That is a waste of time and money. By the time the consultant comes back with the report, the deal is dead or it has gone to someone else—and, in any event, you should not be in a business where you need to rely on consultants. Know your business inside and out, get all the facts, ask people their opinions, and then go with your gut.

We all have instincts. The important thing is to know how to use them. You may have superb academic credentials, but if you don't use your instincts, you might have a hard time getting to and staying at the top. Too many people have stopped trusting their instincts. They cut off a natural sense that we are all born with.

Nobody can explain exactly why or how instinct works. Sometimes we get a gut feeling about what we should or should not do although we can't put a finger on the exact reasons. Most successful businesspeople know they have good instincts and rely on them for making brilliant decisions but rarely understand how it works.

Scientists think that our brains pick up on and somehow perceive the underlying patterns in our daily activities. Then, when we are facing a new situation, we can predict the result because we have seen similar patterns before. I have gotten so used to making deals that I am keenly aware of every nuance of every stage of deal making. I know when someone is stalling for time or is not really serious and is just wasting my time. I know when somebody is lying and I can pick up the telltale signs that something is not right about a deal because it is just too good to be true. I know when my opponent is weak, and I should go in for the kill.

Scientists also say that there are nerve cells in the gut that are connected to the intuitive part of the brain. When something is right or wrong, I actually feel it in my gut. For example, within a few seconds of meeting Mark Burnett, the creator of *The Apprentice*, I realized that I had a very positive gut feeling about him and that I would feel comfortable working with him.

Somehow I knew he was 100 percent solid, both as a person and as a professional. I made my deal with Mark Burnett that very day, without anything but a gut feeling and a solid handshake. On the other hand, I have met people that, for no particular reason, I did not like. I have learned from experience to trust my gut and be wary of those people.

One day I got a call that CBS wanted to use the Wollman Skating Rink, a great place I built and run in Central Park. They wanted to hold a live *Survivor* finale there. I was not sure that was a good idea because it might rain. Then what would we do?

If it rains I would look like an idiot. My hair would be all screwed up. But at least everyone would see it is real. A major newspaper recently ran a great article about me saying, "Trump is brilliant, he's wonderful, he's amazing, but his hairpiece is terrible." It said I wore a hairpiece. Think of it, I had an article in a major newspaper, which was a ten except it said I wear a hairpiece. What a way to ruin an otherwise beautiful article—I couldn't even send it to anyone!

I said okay, and *Survivor* used the Wollman Skating Rink for their finale. Mark Burnett, who I had never met before, was there. I knew he did *Survivor*. We met and talked, and it was quite amazing. I respected him right away. The set the *Survivor* crew built in the Wollman Rink was a jungle that overlooked Manhattan. It was beautiful, and they did a great job.

Mark Burnett said to me, "Donald, Mr. Trump, I'd like to have a meeting with you. I have an idea."

"What's the idea?" I asked.

"I want to do a show with you."

I said, "Well, everybody wants to do a show with me." Other people wanted me to do one of those reality shows where a camera crew follows you. That would not work. I can't have cameras filming me while I am working. I can't have that. So I had turned down many other offers from virtually every other network.

Burnett came to my office the next day and pitched me the show. He told me about the format of *The Apprentice,* and I said, "That's good, because you're not really following me, you're following the kids. I have a boardroom. I rant and rave like a lunatic and the crazier I am, the higher the ratings." So I said, "Okay, I like that idea." We shook hands and that was it. We became fifty-fifty partners.

Then my agent, one of the biggest in Hollywood, called me and said, "I heard you agreed to do this show called *The Apprentice,* a reality show. I don't want you to do it. No business show in the history of television has ever made it in prime time, never once." I said, "You know, you're right." I added, "I have a problem, I shook his hand!" I had agreed and now this guy, my agent, was telling me it was a bad move.

YOUR WORD IS GOLDEN

That is another very important thing: when you shake some-body's hand, go with it. It is very important. Shaking hands with someone means you are making a deal. You are giving your word. If you back out after you have shaken hands on a deal, then people will never trust you again. My agent did not care. He said, "I don't want you to do it!" He called Mark Burnett to tell him the deal was off.

Mark called me up and said, "Your agent called and he's canceling *The Apprentice.*" I said, "Mark, I shook your hand, I don't know if it's good or bad." My agent told me that 98 percent of the shows that go on television fail, which I did not know before I made the deal. I didn't know that no business show has ever made it in prime time. So I went into the deal because I didn't know any better, but something told me this was a good guy and this deal would work out. I had shaken his hand, so I decided to go with it.

Later, after we announced *The Apprentice,* NBC and every network were fighting over it. ABC won, but Michael Eisner tried to better the deal made by his executives so we dropped them and went with NBC which was headed by a really great guy who loved the show, Jeff Zucker. When it went on the air it started at number ten for the first week, which was huge. It then went to number eight, then to number five, and then number three. Finally, it became the number one show on television and its finale, which drew tremendous numbers, was easily the number one show of the week even against strong competition.

All of a sudden I was a freakin' television star. Can you believe that? A real estate guy like me becoming a star? I'll never forget, I went to the upfronts at Lincoln Center for the Performing Arts. All television networks have what they call upfronts where they show off their new season. Big stars were there, Whoopi Goldberg, Rob Lowe, and many others. Not only did my show become number one, every single new show on NBC died except for *The Apprentice*.

After *The Apprentice* became the number one show, I got a call from my agent. He said, "Donald, congratulations. You've just gone to number one. I'd like to come and see you."

I said, "What would you like to see me about?"

He said, "Well, I think I'm entitled to a commission."

Can you believe this shit? I said, "Really, but you were totally opposed to doing it."

"Well, I know that, but I wasn't really that opposed."

I said, "How much commission do you think you should get?"

He said, "I think three million dollars would be appropriate."

I said, "You're fired!"

SOME THINGS WORK BECAUSE YOU DO NOT KNOW THEY ARE IMPOSSIBLE

When NBC agreed to do *The Apprentice* few people thought it would make it. They did not even have an option for a second season. I am the only schmuck who figured it could work because I did not know anything about television.

Then, on my birthday, at 6:30 A.M. I get a call from the chairman of NBC, a fantastic guy named Bob Wright. "Donald, I just called to wish you a happy birthday." I could hardly believe it. Then I get another call at about seven o' clock from the President of NBC, Jeff Zucker, who had the guts to go with *The Apprentice* in the first place. He said, "Donald, I just wanted to wish you a very happy birthday." Then my wife, Melania, rolled over and said, "Who was that?" I said, "Some people from NBC wishing me a happy birthday." She said, "Happy birthday, darling!" Can you believe that? The heads of NBC wished me a happy birthday before seven in the morning?

Not long after, Zucker, who's now CEO of NBC Universal, spoke at a big meeting and said something I will never forget, because *Friends* was in its last season, and *The Apprentice* followed *Friends*. He said very, very nicely, "Donald Trump may not have hair as good as Jennifer Aniston, but he's got great ratings." I didn't mind that he made a crack about my hair because everyone else does.

At that point, I had no agent, I had no contract, and I had a big hit show! NBC was really hot to make a new deal. I had to fend for myself, but I knew I had all of the cards—no entertainment experience, but all of the cards.

About that time, I read an article in the *New York Post* that every member of the *Friends* cast, for the last year, made $2 million per show. There are six characters, and they all stuck together, which was very smart. They each got $2 million per show! When NBC came to see me they said, "We'd like to extend you for a three-year period." I decided I was going to be tough. I thought, "This is going to be fun!" You do not have to be a genius to know that if you have the number one show, you have the network by the you know what.

I said, "I want *Friends*-type money!" I kiddingly slammed my fists on the table—remember these are friends of mine and the NBC people said, "Whoa! We think we can do that." They thought I wanted $2 million an episode like the stars of *Friends*. I said, "No, no, you don't understand. There are six of them and there's only one of me; therefore, I want $12 million a show." They got a little concerned at my request but we made a deal (for much less money) and everybody was happy. It has worked out very nicely for everyone and has been a great success. Now here is a show that was not supposed to work, but it did. It worked because I took a chance. Go with your gut. Take chances. If you think you have the ingredients that you need, take chances, because your biggest successes will happen when you go against the tide; when you take a risk and it works. The NBC people were and are great, Mark Burnett is great and Donald Trump is at least O.K.!

Going with your instincts takes some practice, but first you must decide that you are going to tune in to them. Instincts are a part of every highly charged situation that matters a lot to you and tuning in to them requires extreme focus, like that of a skier navigating a tough slope or an accountant trying to pass the CPA exam. In these do-or-die situations there is not enough time to be 100 percent logical. That is too slow. When time is short and you have big stakes in the game, you have to go with your gut. A blend of logic and instincts will produce the best decisions.

When I was acquiring 40 Wall Street, literally every person I met with recommended that it be turned into residential units, but I did not agree. My gut instincts told me it was a great business location. I trusted my instincts and the building now houses many thriving businesses. It has been a lucrative deal!

When I first started building golf courses, my instincts told me it was a good business decision. I knew if I combined my passion for golf with my knowledge of real estate, I would succeed. I found the best golf course designers in the world and spent many hours working with them. The results have been spectacular because I paired both instinct and logic. But perhaps most importantly, I found the best locations.

Practice listening to your instincts. Play with this skill, and test it out on small decisions. Learn to trust it. You will acquire a real edge in both your business and your personal life. Use this skill to choose who you date and who you trust to babysit your children—which are truly important decisions.

Many things are hidden from us that we cannot articulate logically, but somehow we know they are there. We have a vague feeling that cannot be explained. This feeling in and of itself is information enough for us to take notice and consider. You can know whether the feeling is good or bad. If you have a good feeling about something, go ahead with it. If the feeling is bad, proceed with caution. Your instincts are there to guide you. Use them.

WHEN ACTION IS BETTER THAN INFORMATION

Andy Grove, the former CEO of Intel, once said, "Dive deep into the data, then trust your gut." I think this best describes my approach to decision making: I dive as deeply as I can into the facts and figures of a difficult situation. I use logic and reason to interpret the data. I make informed estimates based on past history and experience. Then I go with my gut instincts. If I need to wait a few days for more information, I weigh the cost of waiting against the benefit of more information. If I need to act immediately to make significant profits, I act immediately. If it doesn't matter very much if I wait a few days for more results, I wait.

BUT TIMING IS EVERYTHING

Instinct has a lot to do with timing. You have to be patient and wait for your instincts to tell you the best time to make your move. I sometimes think about buying a piece of property or using a certain design style for months or years without acting on it. Then all of a sudden I will get the feeling that it is time. When I start checking around I usually will find that things have changed, an opening is there that was not there before. Instinct alerted me to the opportunity, and if possible, then I act quickly to make it happen.

I have waited for many years to see some things happen. It can be very difficult to wait, especially for someone like me who is impatient to get things done in record time. To make really good decisions you have to learn to wait until the time is right. This is especially true of negotiations. I am very careful not to plunge in too quickly, especially on a deal I really want to close. I never show my cards. I act as if I am not sure I want the deal. Acting uncertain often makes my opponents push their arguments for the deal more strongly, playing right into my hands. It also gives me time to sit back and come up with creative options that help me close a better deal than I could if I just plunged right in. I could negotiate peace in the Middle East—very few other people could.

I am a great tennis fan and I have noticed that the best players are not always the strongest, the fastest, or the most aggressive. Above all else, the best players have incredible timing. It has a lot to do with poise and finely honed instincts. Roger Federer and Pete Sampras, the two best ever, obviously have great skill but also great timing. Players with the skill of great timing are almost invincible. When great players lose this skill they quickly fall by the wayside. I have also noticed that the funniest comedians are successful because of an impeccable sense of timing. All the best comedians use split-second timing to get their audiences rolling with laughter. They are born with it, but it can also be, even if to a lesser extent, developed.

One time I wanted to invest in a large piece of real estate, but something always kept me from making the final move.

Every time I tried, something stopped me from closing the deal. So I put the project on the back burner, just waiting for the right time to give it another try. Months later the property was severely damaged by a huge storm. Everything had looked good, and while my gut said *no,* my logic said *go ahead.* Had I heeded only my logic and pushed ahead without regard to my gut, I would have lost a lot of money. I bought the property later for less money, but at that time my gut instincts had spared me from making a costly mistake. Always listen to your instincts.

I had my eye on 40 Wall Street for years before making a move. I did not let anyone know I was interested in it. In the early 90s I was recovering from my difficult times, and buying 40 Wall Street was one of the first big deals I did in the beginning of my recovery era. I was interested in the beautiful historic building for a long time, but the timing was just not right for me to move on it. Over time my business tempo changed and I made my move. By waiting and watching, then moving only when my instincts told me the time was right, I made a lot of money, and I also got to know a great and brilliant family from Germany, the Hinneberg family, who have become terrific friends. You can make friends by making deals—a wonderful side benefit.

Just because you know about a promising opportunity does

not automatically mean you should pursue it. Knowing which deals to go after is very tricky. All the signs may be there that this will be a good deal, but that is not enough. You have to let it incubate in your mind and take root in your heart. Then, after a while the time will come when you know beyond a doubt that the opportunity is yours. Keep working at it, give it your attention, and when the time is right, do not miss a beat in going for what you want. That is what timing is about.

When you make decisions, you have to use all of your abilities, your brain, your gut, and your analytical powers. My advice is to go with your gut, but do not bet the ranch on it. Be cautious. Get all the facts, because there is always a reason why everyone else is going the other way. Believe me, when you find something good that everyone else is ignoring, such as 40 Wall Street, when you go against the tide, and you get a 1.3-million-square-foot skyscraper for nothing, that is beautiful. I love it— but be very, very careful, because sometimes it can be trouble; it can be really big trouble.

ZANKER'S TAKE

When I started The Learning Annex I used my gut. And still today I use my gut to pick a lot of the topics and speakers we feature. In my job I have to recognize talent before the rest of the world does. You cannot listen to what other people think. You have to think independently or you will never be really good at what you do. It is the same for movie and TV producers: they have to know what people want to see before anyone else recognizes it. If you do the same thing as everybody else and don't have the guts to stick your neck out and be different, you will at best achieve mediocre success. But more than likely you will fail. So dare to be different. Dare to be unique. And dare to take a chance on something that is unknown.

In 1980 I was among the first people to walk over hot coals with the phenomenal peak-performance guru Tony Robbins. And I did everything I could to promote him because I had a strong conviction that this guy was on to something and would be very big. Tony was one of my biggest finds. I learned a lot from Tony about overcoming fear and stepping up to a much higher level of performance. He got me thinking much differently. His teaching and inspiration laid the groundwork for me to eventually have the guts to go after someone as big as Donald Trump. I give Tony a lot of credit for getting me to find my own passion in business and in my relationships. Go see Tony Robbins at one of my Wealth Expos or at one of Tony's own events. He is definitely life changing. Go to TonyRobbins.com.

In 1981 I had the opportunity to see Deepak Chopra, co-founder of the Chopra Center for Well Being, speak to a small group of thirty-three people in New York. Nobody knew who he was, but I saw immediately that this guy was going to be very successful. I do not know why, but I just had a strong gut feeling about him. He went on to be one of the most well-known and successful mind-and-body doctors of our time.

Although many people ignore this tool, their instincts, I believe everybody has them. It is really just an intelligent response to situations we have experienced before. The more experience we have, the better we are at using our guts. It is like the poker pro who sizes up the situation and decides his next move with a quick glance at his cards and his opponents' faces. We get a gut feeling of what we should or should not do, although we can't put a finger on the exact reasons why.

By 2001, The Learning Annex had been around for over twenty years, and I no longer owned it. It was an old brand, but I started looking at it again and felt there was tremendous untapped potential. Sometimes you see a business and you know in your gut that you can take it to the next level. I trusted my gut, but the problem was that the then-owner of The Learning Annex wanted more cash for the business than I had at the time.

I tried to raise the money to buy back The Learning Annex, but banks and private lenders weren't interested. I believed in my gut, and I sat down with my wife and told her, "Honey, I have to do this." She saw that I had the passion necessary and that there was no stopping me, so she went along with my gut. I took out a second mortgage on our house, maxed out my credit cards, and begged and borrowed from friends and family members, but I was still coming up short. So I flew out to the West Coast to see The Learning Annex owner, and I convinced him to take a note for one year.

Six years later, it is there for everybody to see. The Learning Annex has been on the *Inc.* magazine 500 list of fastest growing companies. My bet was successful. My gut was right.

We were running loads of "real estate" and "how to make money" classes when I bought back The Learning Annex. I started noticing that more and more people were attending. It made sense. I went to high school, I went to college, and no one taught me how to make money. What a gap in our education system. One of the most important things people need in life, and our schools were not teaching it. Students were flocking to these classes. After watching these classes explode, I gathered my team and said, "Let's create an expo filled with these types of classes and get the greatest minds together for one weekend to teach students how to get rich." No one had done this before. My gut told me that if we do it right, it would be big. But my gut was based on the numbers I was seeing. I could have hired consultants, or had my accounting firm do an analysis, but I just knew the time was right.

If you are good at what you do, and analyze the numbers without prejudice, your gut should be working overtime giving you the right decisions. And when you're not sure, just wait. Sometimes I have a feeling about something, so I go to my team and ask them what they feel. What I am really doing is seeing if their gut is telling them something doesn't smell right also. Even when I am not sure what is bothering me, after we brainstorm for a few minutes, I will figure out the issue.

My Vice President, Samantha Del Canto, sometimes in the morning will walk in with her coffee still in her hand, and tell me an issue she is wrestling with, and say, "What does your gut say?" Or sometimes I will walk into her office and tell her I have a bad feeling about a marketing piece or a new speaker, and she will reassure me by saying, "Zanker, go with your gut. It has got us here so far . . . don't stop listening to it." And that is the key . . . you have to listen to it. . . . we were born with natural instincts that we have been taught NOT to listen to. Wrong. . . . your gut is your best friend in making decisions.

Sure, I use rational analysis and get all the facts before making a big decision. But I have become so accustomed to using my gut, I do not feel satisfied unless I have a strong gut feeling to go with my logical reasons. You can sharpen your gut instincts by using them and playing with them. Many people thrive on data and facts. That is okay. But listen to your gut. We had a lawyer once who just analyzed and analyzed data. Brilliant guy, but education numbed his gut and he was in paralysis. He is no longer my lawyer. I couldn't work with him. Just too much analysis. He would give me pages and pages on every side of the issue . . . but when I would ask him the simple question, "What do you think?" He was dumbfounded as if it was a silly question.

After you have gotten all the information related to the decision at hand that you can get, take a break. Do something unrelated to your decision. Take a nap, watch *Seinfeld* reruns, jog around the park. Give your subconscious a chance to toss things around. Then come back to your decision. You will be much more instinctual.

TO SUM IT UP

Develop your gut instincts and act on them. You will have your biggest successes when you go with your gut. Nobody knows everything. Nobody truly knows what the future will bring. When you become knowledgeable about your field, you start picking up the intangible cues and hints about events and people. You will learn to read between the lines and get a sixth sense. Hone this skill and use it wisely, and you will be very successful. Sure, study all the facts and rationally analyze every situation before acting. When it is time to decide, go with your gut.

KEY POINTS

▶ You need really good instincts to make the best decisions.

▶ With experience, you can learn to go with your gut.

▶ When you shake hands with somebody, you make a deal, so keep your word.

▶ Going with your instincts requires tuning in to everything around your decision.

▶ Use instinct to perfect timing.

▶ Get all the facts, then go with your gut.

4

CREATING LUCK

Let's talk about a concept that is very, very complex. It is called "luck." Some people are luckier than others. Some women are born very beautiful. They did not do anything; they were just lucky. Some people have an easy time making it big in business. They are just lucky. Some people try hard, but things always go wrong. It does not seem fair, but I believe in life there is such a thing as luck.

I have a friend who is one of the most important businessmen in the world. He says, "Donald, there's no such thing as luck. You make your own luck."

I said, "Really? You had two great parents, and you were born in the greatest country in the world. Don't you think that's lucky? You were born with a great brain, you're very smart. Don't you think that's lucky?"

"I'm telling you, you make your own luck."

I said, "That's wrong. Some people are just lucky." He is stubborn and I cannot talk him out of it. Nevertheless, the fact is some people *are* luckier than others.

For instance, Billy, a very close friend of mine, is very un-lucky. He is accident prone. I called him not too long ago, and said, "How are you?"

He said, "Not good."

"Oh!" I said, "What the hell is wrong with you?"

"I broke my shoulder."

"You broke your shoulder? How did you break your shoul-der? What are you, a football player?"

He said, "No, I was in an accident. I fell down the stairs, and I broke my shoulder. Oh, I'm in such pain."

As it turns out, the guy was in the hospital. When I went over to see him, he was lying there groaning, his wife was crying, everything was a mess. I said, "Billy, you're going to get out and you'll be just fine." Three weeks later he left the hospital.

While riding home, he got into an automobile accident. A huge truck rammed into one of the big pillars that hold up the signs over the Long Island Expressway, and the sign fell down on top of Billy's car. Whoever heard of such a thing? He had to go back to the hospital. Some people are luckier than others.

About ten years ago I almost got blindsided by a deal that would have put me in the poorhouse. I was really hot about buying a newspaper. I was extremely excited. I had negotiated what I thought was a great deal and would make me a lot of money.

I went around telling everyone I knew how great this deal was. The closing was all set when I unexpectedly came down with a wicked case of the flu. I felt terrible. It was so bad that I called the sellers and told them we would have to postpone the closing until I was better.

This was very unusual. I never get the flu. It's been ten years and I haven't been sick a day since then. As it turned out, the seller called me back and told me he was selling to another buyer. I lost the deal. I'm lucky I did, because that newspaper is worth a lot less now than I was going to pay. I would have lost a fortune on that deal. Catching the flu was a lucky break that saved me from ruin. Sometimes luck makes better deals than talent.

I have watched the great deal-makers for over twenty years, and it is always the same people who are successful. For years and years it has been the same people and the same success. For some reason, some people always seem to be more success-ful than others, guys like Warren Buffett, Steve Schwarzman, Carl Icahn, Henry Kravis, Terry Lundgren of Macy's, John Mack of Morgan Stanley, Stan O'Neil of Merrill Lynch. It does not mean they are smarter, but they are almost always suc-cessful.

CREATE YOUR OWN LUCK

You can do things to help your luck along. Look at Gary Player, the famous golfer. Gary Player is a small person. Years ago in 1978 I saw him win the Masters golf championship. He has won nine majors in his career, even though he is smaller in stature. He has one advantage: he works harder. He always works. He is always exercising and working on his golf swing and his putting skills, while other guys who are twice his size are home watching television. He is the hardest working golfer ever. That is the reason Gary Player won the Masters three times, and has won many other tournaments. When someone asked him, how could he be so lucky? He said, "The harder I work, the luckier I get." That is a great statement. Think about it, highlight it in this book: "The harder I work, the luckier I get."

Gary Player, a great player, they used to call him "diminutive." He was always smaller than everybody else, but he practiced harder than everyone else and he won nine majors. Think of it, he has won nine majors and the commentators would always say, as he walks up to the tee, "the diminutive Gary." How would you like that? You are on television being called diminutive. Not good, but Gary did not care. He would do push-ups every morning, he would do hours of exercise, before anyone else in golf had even heard of exercising regularly. I'll never forget when I saw him win the U.S. Open: he hit an incredible five-iron shot, right next to the pin, sunk it, and won the tournament. The commentators said, "Gary, unbelievable, you got so lucky." He said, "The harder I work, the luckier I get." I just love that statement. Gary is a great guy.

Let me tell you a story about my own life that illustrates the concept that the harder a person works, the luckier he or she gets. Pay close attention because this particular story is a combination of passion, instinct, and, yes . . . luck!

Back in 1991 the markets were terrible, and everyone was going out of business. I was in deep, deep trouble. I owed billions of dollars. Sure, I could tell you all I want about how I handle pressure well, but I owed many banks billions of dollars. It was not exactly fun. Believe me, it is not cool to be Donald Trump when you owe billions of dollars.

One day I was in my office working, and my secretary told me, "Oh, tonight, Mr. Trump, you have a bankers' convention." The black-tie dinner, which I usually attend, was being held at the Waldorf-Astoria Hotel for 2,000 people in the banking industry. When you are in bad times, you do not have the same energy or spirit you have when things are booming. Instead of going out with a bunch of bankers, I wanted to go home and watch a football game on television. I was tired. I had had a terrible day, with banks coming at me from fifteen different angles.

There was one bank in particular that was worse than any of the others. The guy in charge of collecting the loans was mean and nasty. He was putting everybody out of business. He forced thirty-seven real estate people in New York City into bankruptcy by calling in their loans. I owed him around $149 million, which was one of my smaller loans, and I was next on his list. Usually, you can work things out with banks. This guy wanted 100 percent of his money, right now. The guy was an animal. He wanted to destroy me.

I did not want to be with bankers, because when you owe them money, they hate you. Who wants to go to a dinner where every guy in the room wants to clobber you? All the bankers to whom I owed money would be there. It was a cold and rainy night, and I could not take my limo because it would be very uncool to show up at a bankers' meeting, riding in an expensive limo when I owed billions. I was already very tired. When my secretary told me that I had to go to the Waldorf-Astoria, I said, "I'm not going."

I went home, but when I got home I got a second wind, and I said, "You know what? I think I'll go." At the last moment, I put on my tuxedo and went. There were no available cabs, so I had to walk to the hotel, ten blocks from Trump

Tower, in the freezing rain. By the time I got there I was soaked. I felt then as if I had reached my lowest point, but I went because it was my job. When I got there I sat down at a table. There was a banker on my left, a nice guy named Steven. I said, "Hello, Steven, how are you?" Obviously I did not owe him any money, because he was very nice to me. It is easier when you do not owe money. Very nicely he said, "Hello, Donald."

Then I turned to the guy on my right, and I said, "Hello." He just grunted and gave me a dirty look. Then Steven said, "I don't think that guy likes you very much, whoever he is." I did not know the man. He did not even give me his name. He was just an angry person.

I continued talking to Steven for a little while. After a few minutes I tried to talk to the guy on my right again. But it was no use. It was like talking to a stone wall. He made it very clear that he had no use for me. It got really intense. I was miserable, because I hated being in the position where I owed money to just about every banker in New York. That guy was a banker, and he hated me. I figured that I must have owed him a lot of money for him to act that way.

I spent a miserable fifteen minutes trying to communicate. Steven on my left commented, "Man, that guy is nasty," but I kept trying to get something going with the nasty guy. After another fifteen minutes of misery the guy finally started to open up and talk to me a little bit. Then we started to get along a little. Finally, I asked, "What bank are you with?" He told me and I couldn't believe it. I said, "Holy crap. What's your name?" He told me his name, and now I really couldn't believe it. Out of all the people to sit next to in this crowd of 2,000 bankers, I end up sitting right next to the brutal killer who had pulverized so many people and destroyed their lives. He was the killer who was after me. What luck! I was not sure whether it was good luck or bad, but to be sitting right next to this guy was amazing.

I said, "You're the one that's killing everybody, and you want to kill me, too." He said, "Yes, we do," but we kept on talking and after an hour, I was actually getting along with him. He really loves women and wanted to talk about women. So I talked to him about women. Frankly, when you owe someone as much money as I owed him, you talk about whatever they want to talk about.

In talking to him I found out that he was in a lot of trouble himself. He had thrown thirty-seven companies into bankruptcy. Those thirty-seven real estate guys owed him a lot of money and had no way to pay up. Being the mean vicious guy that he was, he wanted blood. Sure, putting thirty-seven companies into bankruptcy made him feel better, but it was not bringing in any money.

In fact he was losing money. His legal fees were eating him

alive, and all his assets were being wiped out. By the way, that is the one good thing about lawyers. Eventually they get so greedy that their client just wants to get out of the case, which is a good time to settle. It turns out that the banker's lawyers had been giving him a dose of his own medicine and his bank was getting hurt financially. His bosses at the bank were angry with him because he was spending too much money on lawyers instead of working out deals that would bring in money.

I was very fortunate to be dealing with him right then. If I had met him a year before, we would not have had a discussion. The year before, he was in no mood to talk; he just wanted to crush everybody in sight. We started getting along and by the end of the evening we were actually enjoying ourselves. Then he said, "You know, Donald, you're not a bad guy!" I said, "I told you!" He said, "How about this? How about you come to my office to work this out."

When things were booming, I was the king, and people came to see me in *my* office. However, when you owe someone money, you go to their office. I could not say, "No, you come up to my office." So this barbarian banker said, "So, how about you come to my office on Monday morning at nine. Let's see if we can work something out." I said, "I'd love that." Monday morning I went to his office, and in five minutes we had worked out a great deal.

That is why I believe in the Gary Player statement, "The harder I work, the luckier I get." I did not want to go out that night. I wanted to stay home. I wanted to relax. I wanted to watch television. I wanted to take it easy. I wanted to do anything but go out with bankers, but I went out with those bankers and I sat next to that difficult guy. If I had not gone out that night, I probably would not be in the situation I am in right now. I probably would not be doing very well right now, like many of the people who went bankrupt and went out of business. If I had not gone to the bankers' convention, that bank would have tried to destroy me (although I would have hit them hard), and I would not be telling you this story.

Going to the bankers' dinner was hard work. It was not like going out to a nice dinner and having a wonderful time; it was work. That was a horrible time in my life, but in the end it all worked out because I did my work, and then I got very lucky, and I worked out an unbelievable deal.

It is true that some people are luckier than others. I have no doubt about that. You can help create your own luck, you can make things happen through hard work and intelligence. You can become luckier. The fact is, plenty of people have been able to take a bad situation or an unlucky situation and turn it around through hard work.

I started building mixed-use hotel-condominiums in New

York City. The strategy has been very successful for me. When I built the Trump International Hotel & Tower in Las Vegas, I knew Las Vegas was a hot market, but I was surprised when the tower sold out before it was even built. I had great luck and perfect timing with that project. I also met another great friend on that deal, Phil Ruffin, a guy who has made a fortune and truly has great instincts.

Luck does not come around often. So when it does, be sure to take full advantage of it, even if it means working very hard. When luck is on your side it is not the time to be modest or timid. It is the time to go for the biggest success you can possibly achieve. That is the true meaning of thinking big.

GOOD LUCK HAPPENS WHEN OPPORTUNITY MEETS PREPARATION

The past few years of my life have been very active, to put it mildly. The pace has escalated to enormous proportions. I love it that way. It is extremely demanding but also very fulfilling and exciting. I am no stranger to working hard. I have done it all my life. As a result I have become accustomed to expecting success in everything I do. Some people call me lucky, but I know better. Like Gary Player said, work has a lot to do with it.

A lot of people look at successful people and do not see anything but the end result. They do not see all the work that went into getting there. Then they attribute all that success to luck. I look at it this way: I say, "Sure, they were lucky; they were lucky enough to have the brains to work hard."

For example, when *The Apprentice* became a big hit everybody thought I was lucky, but I had over thirty years of experience to draw from in those boardroom scenes. I come across as someone who knows what he is doing because I have been there myself. *The Apprentice* gives people a real taste of being inside a high-stakes New York corporation, which appeals to many people. Being on television was new to me, but the rest was not particularly new. Business is business, whether it is being filmed or not.

I have written a lot of books, and lately it seems like I am always writing a book. I spend up to seven or eight months putting together notes, collecting articles, and dictating stories and ideas before I even start writing. Then there is writing and editing. The whole endeavor of creating a finished manuscript takes a lot of time, patience, and persistence, but when I see the first printed copies come off the press, I feel a wave of satisfaction at a job well done. Readers never see all the sweat and muscle that goes into a book, but books do not just appear out of nowhere.

While I was in the process of writing one of my books, I became interested in the origins of the new "give me" attitude that seems to be sweeping across this country. I believe it started in the late 80s with the emergence of the instant gratification ethic of the "me" generation. Young people graduated from college expecting to be instantly successful. That mentality continued into the 90s spurred by the tech bubble and the booming stock market.

People in their twenties were quitting their jobs to join start-up tech companies and become multimillionaires or billionaires literally overnight. The old idea of having to work long and hard for success was replaced by an "I want it all right now" attitude. The trend is cemented into the American psyche by the superstar athletes, movie stars, and rock stars on MTV who make tremendous amounts of money and some of them are only in their teens.

Now everyone thinks they should have what those very few people have. The general public is bombarded by media stories of easy success and thinks it should happen that way for them, too. The reality is that this kind of success is rare and happens to only a few people, and it almost never happens overnight. Not everybody can be a Sergey Brin or Jerry Yang, the founders of Yahoo!.

The media has a distorted reality, so that people who have

to struggle or work for long years to be successful are left with a strange feeling that somehow they are being left out. They feel that the world owes them something. In real life it does not work that way. There are no guarantees that anyone will be rich and successful. Nobody owes you anything. You need to get down to earth and realize that you have to pave your own way to success by working hard and being diligent. There is no other way.

Sure, luck plays some part in the scheme of things. No question, but you cannot control luck. All you can do is to look at what you have going for you, and use it to the max! Ignore what you lack. If you dwell on the negative, it is all over for you. Luck will not have a chance to show up in your life. Remember, many people have made it big in spite of their weaknesses. It is very important to know what you want for yourself, not what other people want for you. Make your own decisions on what is best for you.

DO NOT BE AFRAID TO TAKE CHANCES

Keeping your nose to the grindstone does not mean that you should let yourself get stale. Be open to new ideas and be willing to try new things. What if I had said "I don't want my name out there" when asked if I would add the Trump trademark to products other than my buildings? I was presented with various opportunities to lend my name to many products and because I was willing to try new things, the Trump name is on the highest quality suits, ties, shirts, vodka, steaks, and so on. I was proud to get behind all of the products, and they are successful. If I were not willing to try something new, these things would not exist.

When I was presented with the opportunity to build my first golf course, I had to think it over carefully. It was an exciting opportunity to build something I had never built before. It was a chance to flex my muscles and create something new that was both functional and awe-inspiring. I hesitated because it was new territory for me and I had a lot to learn.

I decided to go ahead with it. Some people asked me why I was bothering to get involved with building golf courses. I did not need the work or the money. I had plenty of other ventures to work on that I knew could and would not have to take the trouble to learn anything new.

At this time in my life I have the luxury of working on whatever I want. So I decided to work on golf courses because I love to golf, and I wanted to create spectacular courses to play on. I did not need to do it, but I wanted to do it. To me, that was a great reason. As it turned out I had a great time working on golf courses, and it has been very profitable for me as well. It would have never happened if I were not open to new experiences.

I had the same experience when I started *The Apprentice*. I knew nothing at all about television except that for some reason shows like Larry King, Bill O'Reilly, and many others always got high ratings when they put me on—a big point. It was completely new terrain for me, but I was willing to give it a try. I immersed myself in it and discovered that I really enjoyed finding interesting ways to make the show more exciting and appealing to viewers. Look what happened. I never expected it at the start, but I ended up being the star of a monster show on TV. *The Apprentice* went from nothing to a big success with 41.5 million people watching the finale.

The Apprentice was a tremendous hit. Why? Because I took a chance on something brand new. In reality, it was not a big risk. I did not risk my entire fortune on it. Some very smart people had told me that if it failed, it would be a tremendous blow to my image. I said, "My image is so freakin' bad, what the hell difference does it make?"

I can't emphasize enough how important it is to take chances on something new. Recently, my friend Vince McMahon invited me to take part in a huge WWE WrestleMania event called the Battle of the Billionaires. While I like to watch wrestling, I had never actually considered participating; it was totally out of character for me. I said, "What the hell. Why don't I give it a try? What do I have to lose?" So I took a chance and told Vince I would do it. Vince McMahon is an amazing guy and he puts on an unbelievable show.

A record 82,000 people filled the football stadium where the Detroit Lions play to see the Battle of the Billionaires.

Vince and I selected wrestlers to represent us in the ring. If my guy lost, Vince would get to shave my head in front of 82,000 screaming fans. If Vince's guy lost, I would get to shave his head. Vince chose a 400-pound Samoan named Umaga. I chose Bobby Lashley, who is 310 pounds of solid muscle.

It was a great fight, and the two wrestlers really went at it. When my guy won, I could not wait to pin Vince down and shave his head. In front of all the people in the stadium and the millions watching from home, I got to shave Vince's head. I ran him down and tackled him, and then I punched him a few times in the head. Then a wrestler came and held him down while I shaved off all his hair. Later, when I least expected it, Stone Cold Steve Austin came up and gave me a good whomping, just to get even. It was all done in great fun. I had a great time and Vince broke all records—both television and live attendance.

The job that Vince and his crew did was unbelievable. Even

The New York Times did a major piece on the fact that it was so successful. I am glad I took a chance and did something out of the ordinary for me. Fortunately, taking a risk paid off extremely well. The event generated a lot of buzz, it was a blast, and, most important, I got to keep my hair.

When you are focusing on a career, it is easy to get in a rut and not allow yourself to try new things. After a while we are so bogged down by routine we are afraid to try new things. Do not let that happen to you. Be willing to step out of your comfort zone and do things you have never done before. It will give you a new perspective on life that will apply to everything you do. My experience building golf courses and participating in a television show has opened up a new world for me, giving me new challenges and new opportunities to use my intelligence and creativity in different ways.

Always remain open to new ideas, information, and opportunities. Do not close your mind to new things, thinking that you know everything you need to know. The world is rapidly changing, and you must keep on top of things if you want to succeed. It is just plain stupid to put on blinders when faced with new discoveries and opportunities. When I started in business I was successful primarily because I was alert to new ideas and hidden opportunities.

Being alert and open is how I found my best deals and

made the most money. If I had closed my eyes to what was going on around me, I would have never made it. I would have been finished before I began. Do not make that mistake. Every business has surprises, hidden dangers beneath the surface, and little-known opportunities that can lead to a huge success.

I start each day very early in the morning by reading newspapers. I do not read with any particular goal in mind except to satisfy my thirst for knowledge. I read widely on many topics, not just about business, but for the fun of learning interesting new things. It is a terrific way to start the day. When I learn, it makes me feel great, alive, and excited. It makes me want to learn more. As a result, I am never bored, which I think is a big reason for my success.

DEVELOP POSITIVE STAMINA

Another thing you can do is to think positively and expect the best. My positive attitude has brought me a lot of luck. In the very beginning of my career, when I was trying to buy the huge abandoned Penn Central rail yard on Manhattan's West Side, I was new to the city. I had no money, no employees, and no contacts. The city was in the middle of a financial crisis, but I was optimistic and enthusiastic. Because I was so young I could not sell the banks on my experience or my accomplishments, so I sold them on my enthusiasm.

It is important to think positively. Negative thinking, especially about yourself and about your prospects for success, will kill your focus and destroy any chance you have of being successful. I play golf, and I have noticed that the best golfers are the ones who have the greatest ability to think positively. It is not about how far or how straight you can hit the ball—golf is not really a physical game, it is a mental game. The best golfers are mentally tough. Golf is designed to test your mental toughness in the most adverse situations. Trees, roughs, sand traps, bunkers, water hazards, and doglegs are there to intimidate you and make you lose your mental concentration.

So, learn how to manage your mind. Do not let a situation lure you into thinking negatively, sometimes you will fail, but you will learn for the next time. Every time a negative thought comes at you, zap it. Replace it with a positive thought. That takes energy, but the result will be stamina—positive stamina, a necessary ingredient for success.

Do not give in to anger. Many people think I am an angry guy. But it's not true. I am tough and I am demanding, but I never lose it. Sure, you have to be tough, but out-of-control anger is not toughness, it is weakness. It destroys your focus on goals and ruins your concentration.

When I feel angry, instead of letting it out, I channel that energy into activities. I work harder, concentrate more, or bolster my will and my resolve in overcoming a difficult problem, instead of just losing my temper. Sometimes I use anger in a controlled way to make a point when I am negotiating. In those situations, I am using anger for an effect, to further my goals. Using anger constructively is another form of mental toughness that you need to succeed. If you are tempted to blow off steam, you should put that steam into getting the things you want.

Positive thinking is not merely wishful thinking. It is all about incorporating a sense of optimism into everything you do while also acknowledging the negative. Former British prime minister Winston Churchill had this kind of optimism even though he faced a major challenge to England's very survival. President Ronald Reagan, too, was a sunny optimist in the midst of a frightening cold war when the world could have been blown to smithereens on a whim. Reagan knew the dangers, yet he stayed positive, and he triumphed and left a great legacy. Learn how to be optimistic even in the face of large and intimidating challenges and it will revolutionize your life.

My inherent optimism led me to do *The Apprentice*. I did not automatically say no when I was asked to do the show. I had turned down other invitations to do business-based reality shows, but out of optimism I considered this one. When I heard the idea I felt optimistic that the show could succeed. It was the first television idea that ever excited me.

I knew doing *The Apprentice* was a risk. Everybody told me that "most new TV shows fail" or "reality TV is on the way out" or "you will lose your credibility." I thought about it carefully and weighed all the risks by asking "what if" questions. What if it were a success? What if I enjoyed it? What if it proved to be enlightening? What if it brought the Trump Organization more of the recognition it deserved? What if the job provided to the winner proved to be a valuable stepping-stone for a deserving individual?

By the end of this thought process, I had a long list of positives to go along with the negatives. So I decided to do it, and it was a great success, and all the positives have come true. If I had only focused on the negatives I would have never done it, and I would not have enjoyed the rewards. Instead, I chose a positive perspective.

At a very young age I read a book *The Power of Positive Thinking* by the great orator and minister Dr. Norman Vincent Peale. There is a popular book out right now called *The Secret*, which is along the same lines: positive thinking. It is a number one bestseller. Some of the experts cited in *The Secret* are speaking at The Learning Annex Wealth Expos with me. I firmly believe in the power of positive thinking.

The lessons in *The Power of Positive Thinking* really stuck with me. In every deal I do, my main job is to be positive, even when everybody else is negative and gloomy. When I bought an option on the West Side properties from Penn Central in the 70s, everybody in the city was gloomy. Every day, headlines in the papers told of bankruptcies and financial collapses of every kind. Nobody knew if the city was even going to survive. I stayed positive and I went around the city talking to people and convincing them to be positive—bankers, city officials, architects, and contractors. I gave them the hope that things would ultimately work out. As the developer, that is my job.

THE POWER OF NEGATIVE THINKING

I also believe in the power of negative thinking. You have to think negatively sometimes. It is sort of like putting up your guard. You need to protect yourself against all the negative forces out there in the world. Whether you like it or not, there are wars, tsunamis, hurricanes, tornados, and bad people. So I practice the power of positive thinking while doing all I reasonably can to protect myself from the bad things.

Here is an example of my negative thinking. When I bought the Commodore Hotel from Penn Central, I was not naive. I knew there were risks. If I failed, the deal would bury me. From the very beginning I tried to keep my risks and my financial exposure to a minimum. I was not such a positive thinker that I opened myself up to unnecessary dangers. I kept everybody who was involved in making the deal—the bankers, Penn Central, and the city—believing that I was the best chance they had to renovate the old dilapidated building and revitalize the entire neighborhood, without my having to risk any hard cash.

Finally, we arrived at a deal in which I got an exclusive option to purchase the property for $10 million subject to the city granting me a tax abatement and me finding financing and a management company to run the hotel. The price of the option was $250,000. I did not have $250,000 that I wanted to risk on this deal. I drew up the contract but did not fork over the $250,000. Instead I had my lawyers find lots of legal points to argue back and forth while I was busy trying to put the rest of the deal together. Be positive, but never go out on a limb for some pie-in-the-sky idea that may or may not pan out.

A truly positive mental attitude is when you are good at what you do and you are prepared for every possibility, both positive and negative. You can boost your positive mental attitude by being thoroughly prepared. You cannot expect to be successful 100 percent of the time no matter whether you are in business, finance, real estate, management, medicine, or science. If you are not prepared for a negative result, a few minor setbacks, the loss of a promotion, or a deal falling through, such an experience will cause you an unnecessary amount of confusion and doubt. Both a positive mental attitude and a good work ethic are important in creating your own luck, but you cannot rely solely on them.

The real-life truth is that deals do not always close, you do not always land the new account, you do not always win the lawsuit, you do not always get the promotion, your patients do not always recover, and the people you deal with are not always honest. There are always circumstances beyond your control. The only way to guard against having your confidence shattered is to come to grips with the stark reality that negative things can and do happen. Count on it. Be prepared for it. Realize that it is life, and that it has nothing to do with you or your abilities. Do not let it shake your self-confidence one iota!

ZANKER'S TAKE

In 1982 an amazing stroke of luck pushed The Learning Annex into the big time real fast. On Thursday, March 11, 1982, I discovered that The Learning Annex had enrolled our one-hundred-thousandth student. I wanted to celebrate this momentous event by throwing 10,000 one-dollar bills off the top of the Empire State Building. It was my way of giving back to the community and getting some much-needed publicity. Despite being severely undercapitalized I decided to take a big chance. My colleagues and I got as many dollar bills as we could at the bank and pasted a label on each bill, which read "The Learning Annex Loves New York."

Then we told all the news media and TV stations about our plan to throw $10,000 off the Empire State Building starting at 1 P.M. on Friday, March 12. They loved this story and alerted all of New York about this incredible way to get some free money. It caught everyone's attention. So that Thursday afternoon we stuffed the 10,000 one-dollar bills into two huge clear garbage bags and the next day we trekked over to the Empire State Building to pass out all the loot. The city had blocked off 34th Street, and thousands of people showed up to collect their money, along with television crews, reporters, photographers, and a squadron of cops to keep order.

But thirty minutes before we got to the Empire State Building two men decided to rob the Bankers Trust branch located on the ground floor of the building. The two robbers entered the bank, vaulted the counter, scooped up a pile of money in garbage bags, and fled. When they exited the bank they were greeted by an amazing spectacle: thousands of bystanders, camera crews, reporters, police officers, and store detectives. The men ran through the crowd pursued by a bank guard and several plainclothes officers shouting "Holdup! Holdup!" Both suspects were quickly apprehended and arrested.

That is when we showed up with the two big garbage bags full of our money. We made our way into the lobby of the building, but authorities wouldn't let us go up the elevator and refused to let us dump our precious cargo. I tried to reason with them, saying, "As far as I know it's not a crime."

They would not budge. So here we were, walking around the crowded lobby holding two huge bags of money over our heads, with people pressing in from all sides trying to get some of it. It was a scary experience. I never got to throw the money. We had to be taken away in a patrol car for our own safety.

This strange turn of events ended up being the biggest break in my career. The next day the bizarre story ended up on the front page of *The New York Times* and thousands of other newspapers around the world. I was asked to be on all the talk shows and it created a huge amount of publicity for The Learning Annex. It was amazingly good luck. I had expected to get some publicity from throwing the dollars from the building, but I never expected a huge front page story. Because the bank robbery happened at the same time as our intended stunt, The Learning Annex got an incredible amount of publicity from the story, and The Learning Annex took off literally overnight, which gave me the cash flow I so sorely needed at that time.

Luck can also come in the form of good timing. Right after I signed Donald Trump to do the first Wealth Expo, the first season of *The Apprentice* was aired on NBC. The publicity around that show was phenomenal! The ratings were through the roof, and everybody was talking about Donald Trump saying the infamous words "You're fired!" Donald Trump became a household name and was talked about at every office water cooler. The number of people who signed up to see The Donald in person at the first expo went through the roof. Obviously it was great timing and great luck.

But here is the most important point: I took the luck that was handed to me and I ran with it. You may get only one or two lucky breaks like that in your life, and when you do, you have to run with it. The first Wealth Expo was a great success. Yet many people were advising me to leave it at that. We made a lot of money, so why do another expo and risk losing all the profits we made? Why don't we stop there?

But I knew one thing from past experience; once you have a stroke of luck, you should keep it going. I decided to immediately go out and schedule twenty more expos in every major city in America.

Likewise, Steve Jobs turned his work into amazing luck. He was motivated to build the first personal computer and wanted to sell them to the general public like Motorola sold TVs. He got together with partner Steve Wozniak and sold his Volkswagen van and Hewlett Packard programmable calculator for $1,350. Using that money, Jobs worked day and night to build the first Apple computer. After taking on this amazing challenge he went from college dropout to the person who started the boom in personal computers that changed all our lives.

Look for something that stimulates you to stretch yourself beyond your normal limits. Then you must work on improving your skills every day and never quit. In just about every field, people learn quickly at first, and then, after a while, they stop learning. Only a few people keep on improving for years and decades; the ones we call great. Winston Churchill is one of the greatest orators of the twentieth century. People believe that he was born that way. But the truth is he practiced his speeches over and over until he got them right. Bobby Fischer became a chess grandmaster at age sixteen. A child prodigy? Hardly. Fischer practiced intensively for nine years before winning his title.

Tiger Woods became the youngest winner ever of the U.S. Amateur Championship at age eighteen. He practiced for a solid fifteen years to get there. Use your work as your practice. Always try to improve on your performance. Do not be satisfied to simply get the job done, aim to improve. If you are a web designer, with every job you do, be more creative. If you write financial reports, strive to top yourself by doing better research, analysis, and presentation with each project. It is the same for engineers, accountants, management consultants, lawyers, teachers, physicians, psychologists, inventors, poets, musicians, builders, and entrepreneurs. Use your work to better yourself. You will get recognized. Make every day extraordinary no matter what your job is.

Work is hard enough without putting forth extra effort. Most people do their jobs on remote control. It is just work. But if you tried every day to take pride in your job and become better and better at it, eventually you will become great and get noticed. Then everyone will say you had good luck.

TO SUM IT UP

Some people are born luckier than others, it's true. Lucky people are born with wealthy parents, good schooling opportunities, and powerful connections that give them an advantage over the rest of us. Most of the supersuccessful people I know worked hard to create their own luck.

Remember, "The harder I work, the luckier I get." One day, in my darkest hour, I went to a bankers' dinner in Manhattan. That one event changed the course of my life. If I had not gone to that dinner, I may not be writing this book. I hated to go to that dinner with bankers. I went because it was my job to go there. It was work, horrible hard work, but I worked hard, and I got lucky; that is why I am here today. You can make luck happen through hard work and intelligence. Sure, bad things can and do happen—be prepared for the worst, but if you work hard and are smart, luck comes your way when you least expect it.

KEY POINTS

▶ Some people are naturally luckier than others, but that is just a small starting point.

▶ You can create your own luck.

▶ The harder you work, the luckier you get.

▶ The world does not owe you anything; you have to work for it.

▶ Good luck does not come overnight.

▶ Be open to new information and ideas.

▶ Be willing to take on new challenges.

▶ Always think positively and expect the best.

▶ Do not let anything get in your way.

▶ Protect your back by thinking negatively.

▶ Stay confident even when something bad happens. It is just a bump in the road. It will pass.

5

FEAR FACTOR

Life is not easy. The world is a vicious, brutal place. It's a place where people are looking to kill you, if not physically, then mentally. In the world that we live in every day it is usually the mental kill. People are looking to put you down, especially if you are on top. When I watched westerns as a kid, I noticed that the cowboys were always trying to kill the fastest gun. As a kid, I never understood it. Why would anyone want to go after the fastest gun?

That is the way it is in real life. Everyone wants to kill the fastest gun. In real estate, I am the fastest gun, and everyone wants to kill me. You have to know how to defend yourself. People will be nasty and try to kill you just for sport. Even your friends are out to get you!

AS SOON AS YOU SUCCEED
THEY ARE COMING AFTER YOU

I own a beautiful club in Florida called The Mar-a-Lago Club. I have had Elton John, Celine Dion, and many others perform there and just about everybody with a lot of money wants to be a member. It has been a great big success. One of my members is a big real estate guy from New York. Three years ago this guy paid me some money and joined my golf club. He is a tough, mean, crude guy, and he is worth about a billion bucks, which today is not such a big amount of money. He's not the wealthiest member, but he's still worth a billion dollars. I always treated him well. I would tell the staff, "Make sure my friend has a good table." Real estate people are like a fraternity. When somebody is in the same business, we take care of each other. That is why I told my staff, "Make sure he gets treated well."

One day I got a call from one of my lawyers about one of the office building deals I had done. He tells me this guy I know who owns a totally different kind of building in a totally different section of New York had sued me. I said, "No way, it is impossible. I treat him great."

I thought that it was impossible that he would sue me. He would never do that because he was a member of my club, and I treat him so well. Nobody gets better treatment. The lawyer insisted, "Mr. Trump, I'm telling you, it is him." I said, "No way, go back and check." He called me back an hour later. He said, "Mr. Trump, it is definitely this guy and his company."

That woke me out of my illusions about him and our happy little fraternity of real estate people. I should have known! This guy was bad news. He was your typical greedy, mean-spirited real estate developer who took great pleasure in nickel-and-diming his adversaries to death.

He sued me for naming rights. He claimed that the name I was using caused confusion with his building. When I got together with my lawyers they told me, "Mr. Trump, it's going to cost a lot of money." Then I called this guy. I said, "Let me ask you something. Is it possible that you just sued me?" He said, "Yes, I did, Donald." I said, "Why?" He said, "There's confusion." I said, "Confusion? There's no way. The names are different, the buildings are different, and they are not located anywhere near each other. So how can you say there is confusion? This is bullshit!" That's how some people are. They come after you just for sport, because they want to bring you down any way they can.

My lawyer studied the situation and came back to me with this advice, "Mr. Trump, you'll win the case, but it will cost you about half a million dollars." I asked "Why is it going to cost so much money?" The lawyer said, "We'll have to go out and do polls that show that the public isn't confused. It's very expensive." I said, "I don't freakin' believe it!" I didn't want to spend all that money, but I figured what the hell. I told them to go ahead and fight the bastard.

My lawyers told his lawyers that we were going to fight him in court. A few days later I got a call from my lawyer telling me that the other side wanted to settle—and all they wanted was free club dues for him for the rest of his life. Do you believe that? In return I can keep using the name on my building, and he can keep using the name on his building, and everybody is happy.

At first I said to myself, "I hate to do it, because of the principle of it." Then I said, "All right, we'll settle." I made a deal because, when you look at it, I would save a lot of money in legal fees. You have a guy who is worth over $1 billion and he's going to save a measly $8,000 a year in dues at my club. Eight thousand dollars! He was being treated like a king, and now he made me his enemy. Maybe he likes it that way.

I made the deal, but from that day on I treated that guy like the worst piece of shit you've ever seen. The amazing thing is, the worse I treat him the more he comes back. It is unbelievable. One night he was at a party at the club and I said to his face in front of ten people at his table, "You piece of garbage, I can't believe you keep coming back." I said to the other people at the table, "How can you sit with a guy like this?" He just sat there and did not say a word.

Two days later he came back. He wanted to find out if he could get tickets for a very popular concert. I told the staff to tell him we were sold out. Whenever he has dinner at the club, which is often, he is seated at the worst table in the worst corner. We treat him like a dog and he comes back for more. It is the most unbelievable thing. It is sick. That's why it is tough in business. I was so naive to think, *no, it couldn't be him*. The fact is, the world is tough and full of ruthless people who attack you for the fun of it, like my so called real estate fraternity brother did. I turned the tables on him though and now I get pleasure out of tormenting that jerk. It just shows that you have to protect yourself even with people that are supposedly your friends. When somebody takes a cheap shot at you do not be afraid to fire back.

You should never sell out your friends. As an example, Donny Deutsch is a great friend of mine. He has a very successful show on CNBC and he also leases an apartment from me on Park Avenue and 59th Street—a new building I built out of the old Delmonico Hotel. It has become very successful and it is one of the hottest buildings in New York. Many people want Donny's apartment either to rent or to buy, but I thought Donny had another two years left on his lease. His rent is

$45,000 a month, so I called Donny and asked when he would be leaving, and he told me "in about two years." So I said, "Okay, I guess I have to wait." The next day his lawyer unexpectedly called my lawyer to tell us that there was a thirty-day termination clause in his lease and they would like to get rid of it. The fact is, because it was not the most important thing on my mind, we did not even know there was a termination clause and had we known we would have terminated him in order to get the much bigger offer.

I now had my people call Donny and explain that we were terminating the lease, but in actuality I was doing it just for fun—as some friends will do! I asked, "I wonder how long it will be before Donny calls me?" Well, the call came in approximately three minutes after notification. He couldn't believe I would do it to him, but I told him, "Donny, your expensive lawyer called and explained to us that we had something that we did not even know we had. Please let me know who this lawyer is, because she made me a lot of money."

In actuality, I would never do anything to hurt him, because (1) he is a great guy and (2) it was really my intent to let him stay for a longer period of time—but I did want to have some fun with him. Donny, rather than getting a much higher rent, agreed to pay me a couple of bucks more, but much more importantly, he agreed to make a $50,000 contribution to one of my favorite charities, the Police Athletic League of New York. So Donny stays in the apartment.

Many strange things happen in business. People you think you know, at least on the outside, turn out to be much different from what you originally thought. I was always of the opinion that Lee Iacocca was a very tough guy, hardnosed in every way. In the 1990s, when real estate markets were crashing, Lee Iacocca wanted to do a deal with me to buy up some property inexpensively, or as we say in real estate, "cheaply."

We looked at a small hotel that he was absolutely in love with in the East 60s, but he was unable to agree on a price.

Later on, a great deal miraculously appeared before me. There were two buildings that cost approximately $139 million to build that went through a bankruptcy and were located in West Palm Beach, Florida. They were beautiful buildings but the real estate "depression" was in full swing and nothing was selling.

The bank that ultimately ended up taking them back, The Bank of New York, really wanted to make a deal. So I bought them with Lee Iacocca. The problem with buying property in a virtual real estate depression is that you have no idea how long the depression will last. If it lasts too long you made a bad bet.

In this case, it lasted for years longer than people antici-pated. Even if you buy the property cheaply, which I did, in the end it's not such a great investment because it takes so long for the market to come back and when you add in the cost of carrying the building and all the costs associated with putting up money early, you're better off just relaxing. In any event, Lee wanted to go into the deal and we did it as a fifty-fifty joint venture.

From the day I made the deal with Lee, he would call me on a daily basis and call the people at the building over and over again. I told him, "Lee, take it easy. It's going to take time. We're in the middle of a virtual real estate depression, and it's not going to go fast. Just take it easy, because time is something we can't do anything about." I had a salesperson working at the job who was very good but also very rough. She had very little regard for Lee and would talk to him in a really tough manner, saying things like, "Why don't you leave us the hell alone? Why do you call so much, what's your problem?" or "Take your face and shove it up your ass." It used to drive him crazy.

In the end, he would call me constantly to see whether he could get out of the deal. It got to a point where he called and it sounded to me like he was crying, I could actually hear him crying, in order to get his money back. This happened on two occasions. I am sure Lee has quite a bit of wealth, so I didn't understand for the relatively small amount he invested (the banks put up most of the money), why he took it so seriously.

One of the more shocking things to happen to me was to hear this man crying who I thought would never shed a tear in his entire life. I ended up giving him back his money and dissolving the partnership. It was easier than putting up with all of his bullshit. Dealing with Lee Iacocca was not fun.

The apartments ultimately sold and today Trump Plaza is 100 percent sold and is one of the highest priced buildings in the Palm Beach area.

WATCH YOUR BACK AND LISTEN

A few years ago, a high-end retail store rented space from me in one of my buildings. They needed to redesign the space before they opened the store. I know every contractor in New York, and only about 25 percent are any good. I know every one of them, because I have been screwed by every one of them. I said to my new tenant, "Don't use a contractor unless I approve it." I really didn't care which contractor they used because they were paying me a huge rent. Since I was not getting a percentage, it didn't matter to me what it ended up costing them, but I like to help people. So I called them and I said, "When you hire your contractor, I recommend the following three people." They said, "Oh, thank you very much."

I called them two months later, and I said, "Who did you use?" They said, "We used so-and-so." I said, "What? He's a total scoundrel. You can't use him. He's going to rip you off." They had a construction budget of $17 million. In New York, $17 million is nothing. This was going to be a big high-end store and they wanted to use a contractor who was going to rip them off.

I'm really smart, and I really know construction. I know this city. There are some terrible people in this city. Now, this contractor that they hired was fired from almost every job that he did, and I believe he had even gone to jail for some terrible things he did.

I said to this tenant, "I am going to do you a tremendous favor. You can't use that guy."

They said, "Why?"

"He'll kill you. Number one, I think he went to jail for stealing. Number two, the job will take twice as long and it will cost you much more than seventeen million dollars."

They said to me, "We're going to use him because we think he's wonderful. We really like him, and by the way, Mr. Trump, we've rented your space, we have a twenty-year lease; we'll do what we want."

I said, "What? You're talking to me that way? You people are stupid." Then I figured they were on their own, and I wouldn't try to help them anymore. That was the first indication I got that their heads weren't on straight.

Then these schmucks came to me with another big problem. The doorway, designed by this big name architect they had hired, was supposed to go right where a column is. I said, "Why don't you change the design and place the door on a wall that hasn't even been built yet. Wouldn't that be a little cheaper?" Moving the column would cost them approximately $2 million. The building would have to be jacked up and then held up while the column was moved. It is a big deal.

In the end, the $17 million renovation they had budgeted ended up costing them $48 million. By that time I was sure those clueless novices would go out of business and that is basically what happened. Finally they came to me and said, "Mr. Trump, we've failed. We want to get out of the lease." I said, "I want you to pay me $100 million to get out of your lease." They said, "We don't have that much." I said, "I'll take less. What do you have?" They named a figure. Believe me it wasn't that much after this contractor was finished with them. I said, "I'll take all of it."

Anyway, it turned out to be a very happy ending. They paid me the money and got out of their lease. That whole experience just shows that you have to be smart and listen. There are many bad people out there who want to take you for every penny you have. If you are stupid and gullible it is only a matter of time before someone takes your money. So watch your step and pay attention.

GET PEOPLE TO RESPECT YOU

You have to make sure that people you deal with know that you know what is happening, because, otherwise, they are really going to take advantage of you. You don't want that to happen. Make them respect you for your knowledge. I am good at real estate. I understand real estate, and I love real estate. Nobody can pull the wool over my eyes when it comes to real estate. That is the most important lesson in getting respect: know your stuff.

Almost from the time I could walk, I had been going to construction sites with my father. I watched him work and I learned how he controlled the men who worked for him. As a teenager, when I came home from military school for vacation, I followed my father around to learn about the business up close: dealing with contractors, inspecting properties, and making deals.

I learned that to make a profit in this business, you have to be able to keep costs down. I learned from my father how to negotiate. My father would negotiate just as hard for mops and brooms as he would in the construction of a building. He knew his stuff. If he knew a roofing job was going to cost the contractor $800,000, then he did not try to beat him down to $600,000. He did not let the roofer push him into paying $1.2 million, either.

You also must let everyone you meet know that you know your stuff. If you are a businessperson, look like a businessperson. Dress the part and act the part. Do not cause any doubt in anybody's mind that you don't know your stuff. When I moved to Manhattan to do my first deal, I did not have money or employees. When I went into an office, I acted as if I had an organization, The Trump Organization, behind me. I was on my own and no longer working for my father. Few people knew that The Trump Organization had no employees except myself and operated out of my studio apartment in Manhattan.

I dressed the part of a successful real estate entrepreneur. I would march into the seller's office, impeccably dressed in my black pin-striped suit, white shirt, and monogrammed tie, armed with the determination and enthusiasm of someone who was going to make things happen. Nobody ever questioned whether I could do it. I acted as if I could do anything, and nobody had the nerve to question that assumption. From the very start I was in complete control of every deal because I commanded everyone's respect.

I was speaking at one of The Learning Annex Expos, and I

was telling the crowd of 62,000 people that I think Secretary of State Condoleezza Rice is a lovely woman, but I'd rather have a bitch negotiating with China and Iran. I'd rather have somebody really tough who's a great negotiator. I used the word *bitch* to describe the type of tough negotiator we need representing the interests of our country. You won't believe what happened. The headline in the paper the next day read, "Trump calls Condi Rice a bitch!" That is not what I said. It just shows that nobody is more dishonest than the press. There are some fine journalists out there, but there are also many scoundrels.

Here is the typical scenario you see over and over again with Condi Rice: She goes to some country to meet a dictator or whatever, who is a ruthless killer, a vicious murderer who is a lot smarter than she is. She walks off an airplane and waves hello with a big smile, and then she does a short sound bite. She goes over to the dictator's office and sits down for a photo op with him. The chairs are set at 45-degree angles so the photographers can get nice pictures of her with the dictator. Then she leaves, waves good-bye, gets back on the airplane, and nothing happens—nothing ever happens.

I could give you the names of ten to twenty of the greatest deal-makers in the world who live in this country. These great negotiators could go up against China or Iran and work out a fabulous deal for the United States. Instead we have well-meaning but naive academic people negotiating, who do not know what they are doing in tough real-life situations. They have never faced tough winner-take-all, fight-to-the-death negotiations against ruthless and vicious adversaries. If the government used our best negotiators, it would solve a lot of our problems and the United States would come out on top. For one thing, we have all the cards: we have the strongest military and the strongest economy on Earth, or at least we had. Who the hell can beat us? We would be negotiating from strength. We would win if we would just sit down and negotiate—but using our best people!

We ought to send one of our top geniuses to negotiate with other countries. Those kinds of people are rare, just like gifted doctors and scientists are rare. I think our enemies are dying to negotiate. How would you like to be Iran right now and not know whether the United States was going to attack? The Iranians are in a tough position. We could make a great deal but we need to have our best people doing the job. Right now nobody is even talking to them. Condi Rice just goes over there to get her picture taken. Such incompetence has got to stop! When you are negotiating or getting someone to do it for you, whether it is for a billion-dollar real estate development, a used car, or an international arms treaty, make sure the people doing the negotiating for you are the best.

DO NOT TRUST ANYONE

I used to say, "Go out and get the best people, and trust them." Over the years I have seen too many shenanigans, and now I say, "Get the best people, and don't trust them." Do not trust them because if you don't know what you are doing, they are going to rob you blind. I know dozens of sophisticated businesspeople who hired accountants and lawyers and others, and they trusted them. They got killed. They lost their businesses. So I say, "Get the best people, and don't trust them."

First, you have to go out and get the best people. Because of *The Apprentice* I now have a public reputation for firing people. The truth is I put much more emphasis on hiring good people and promoting those worthy individuals already working in my company. Over the years I have become a pretty good judge of character.

When I interview people, I try to size them up fairly quickly. I do not waste a lot of time on interviews. I found that every hire is a gamble. All the tests and interviews and wining and dining of new job candidates does not make a bit of difference. I have found that my first impressions are the best guide to selecting good people. Extensive meetings and interviews are often a waste of time.

Sometimes people will come into my office and they will be

great. They will look great, they'll sound great, they dress beautifully; everything is great. Then after you hire them they turn out to be morons. Sometimes a real slob will come in looking for a job. He does not dress well. He does not look good. He does not seem to be very smart. It turns out when you hire him or her, you find out you have hired a genius.

Be careful not to hire people with negative attitudes. The old adage is true: one bad apple can truly spoil the whole barrel. A person with a negative attitude can spread negative feelings like a dangerous virus, bringing down the rest of the office and destroying an otherwise healthy and well-functioning team.

Researchers have proven that negative behavior can hurt a company more than positive behavior can help it. I've found this very interesting and it's very true in my experience. A few negative people can ruin an entire office environment, which shows you how powerful negativity is. It is so bad, even positive workers can't "unspoil" it. If one person is constantly fault-finding, they soon pollute those people who sit and listen to the continuous stream of complaints. Soon the whole office is filled with that person's air of negativity, and it becomes an unpleasant place to work. Everybody who works there feels it. The bad apple's negativity spreads like a cancer and before long everybody is complaining. Even the people who deal with your employees pick up on it, and that is not good for business.

When interviewing new employees, be on the lookout for potential bad apples. If someone complains about their previous job, their employer, or the people they worked with, that is a sign that you will be the target of their complaints if you hire them. When you are hiring, avoid people who in general appear combative or disagreeable. It is a sure omen of future negativity.

I try to hire people who are honest and loyal. I value loyalty very much. I like people who are candid about themselves and are honest and down to earth. I avoid people with especially high opinions of their own abilities or worth. Self-confidence is a good thing, to be pretentious is not.

I am not a conceited person and I do not like to have conceited people around me. People are too busy to cater to that kind of person. My advice is to find people who like to work hard, are willing to learn, are loyal, and welcome challenges. It is not easy to recognize these qualities in people you do not know, so I usually rely on my gut instincts to guide me.

For example, I'm very good at recognizing when someone is conning me. Because of the kind of business I am in, I know instantly when someone is "bullshitting" me. I can spot dishonesty a mile away. Oftentimes an applicant tells me he or she is interested in construction and real estate. Later in the interview I ask him or her about interest rates or variable mortgages, things that anyone remotely interested in real estate would know, and I can tell if the person does not have a clue about what I am saying. That disqualifies the person immediately. When a job applicant is not on the up-and-up with me, I immediately write him or her off.

Some people are smooth like con artists and have a very good delivery. They look the look and talk the talk. It is much harder to tell the phonies from the real McCoys. I try to get them to relax and talk honestly about themselves and their interests. Oftentimes they reveal the truth about what really turns them on and sometimes it is not real estate. They are frustrated musicians or writers going into real estate just for the money. Then it is clear they fit somewhere else, not in real estate. I do not hire those people.

Sometimes candidates look really bad and have little experience, but I can tell that they honestly love real estate and have the drive to work hard doing deals and managing projects. Attitude tells me a lot. If they have the right attitude, they have gotten over the first hurdle with me. After that it is a matter of finding out whether they have the smarts. I have found that tests scores and grades are of little use to me. The people with the best grades are not always the smartest. It is where they go with their gut that really matters. I am used to dealing with really smart people. I have a feel for it. If the person feels like the people I deal with, if they feel smart, then I hire them. It does not always work out, but it is the best way I have found to judge someone's intelligence.

Once you hire a good staff, you still have to manage them. One of the keys to being a great leader is the ability to delegate. For some people, that is not an easy thing to do. It is often difficult to relinquish the reins because you want to make sure things are done correctly. Many people adamantly believe the adage "If you want something done right, you have to do it yourself."

Executives and managers and leaders of any kind are too busy to tend to every detail, so delegation is crucial. However, in order to assign tasks to others, you have to keep track of the people who work for you. They must respect or even fear you, or things will go very wrong. If you are worried about being liked, you are in trouble. It is more important to be respected and feared than to be liked by employees. Creating a company climate where employees respect you and are loyal to you is important for keeping employees in line.

If you do not create an atmosphere of respect and loyalty, you will be in for a struggle. I am sure the executives at Coca-Cola are still reeling over the secretary who was accused of trying to sell company trade secrets to the competitors over at Pepsi.

Fortunately, the executives at Pepsi were honorable and immediately turned her in. She and her accomplices were busted and now face serious charges. It is lucky for Coke that Pepsi did the right thing, and I have a lot of respect for the people at Pepsi for doing it. A lot of competitors might have played a lot dirtier.

The case has made Coke and other corporations re-evaluate how to keep sensitive company information safe. It has also made them look more closely at the screening process for hiring. Everybody is careful when they hire somebody who is going to handle payroll, someone who is going to be writing checks, but you need to be just as careful when you hire someone who is going to have access to your company's most critical information—whether it is a vice president or a receptionist.

One other way to avoid the problem of betrayal is to make all your employees feel like part of the team—if they all feel as if they have a vested interest in the overall success of your business, then, most likely, these situations will not happen.

Here is a great example: It is the story of one employee who is really committed to his job, and he is a great role model for anyone to follow. Recently, New York Yankees player Hideki Matsui injured his wrist during a diving catch in a game against the Boston Red Sox. Unfortunately, the Yankees ended up losing the game. Matsui's injury ended his 1,768-game playing streak that included 1,250 games with the Yomiuri Giants in Japan.

When Matsui was told he probably would have to sit out most of the season, he did not throw a tantrum, curse, or sulk. The first thing he did was apologize. He said, "I feel very sorry and, at the same time, very disappointed to have let my teammates down. I will do my best to fully recover and return to the field to help my team once again."

Joe Torre is a great manager and leader, and he is a friend of mine. When I talked to him, he told me that he was not surprised by Matsui's apology. He said Matsui has apologized in the past whenever he's made an error during a game. Matsui also expressed his appreciation for Yankees manager Joe Torre. He thanked him for putting him in the lineup every day, which had enabled him to keep his playing streak alive that long. Wouldn't it be great if every employee felt that way about his or her job? Suppose all your employees had that kind of attitude and displayed that kind of loyalty. It is certainly an ideal to strive for.

As a matter of fact, I value loyalty above everything else— more than brains, more than drive, and more than energy. On an episode of the fourth season of *The Apprentice,* I was asked why I didn't fire Rebecca Jarvis after the fierce exchange we had in the boardroom.

Rebecca volunteered to be project manager of the women's

team even though she had broken her ankle the week before. I guess she wanted to prove to me how tough she was and that she could lead her team effectively in spite of her handicap. I was impressed with her willingness to take the risk. Unfortunately for her, the gamble did not pay off, and her team lost. In the boardroom all hell broke loose: everybody on Rebecca's team was trying to stay alive by shifting the blame onto someone else.

Many of her team members blamed Toral Mehta's poor performance for the team's loss. Rebecca however steadfastly stood behind Toral, because Toral had helped her with her ankle, and she admired Toral for having graduated from my alma mater, the Wharton School of Finance. Rebecca knew her teammates were right. Instead of sending Toral with her to the boardroom where Toral would most certainly be fired, Rebecca sent her back to the suite.

I personally suggested that she take Toral to the boardroom with her, but Rebecca would not budge. By sticking with Toral she showed a great amount of loyalty. It turned out to be a really smart move. I wanted to fire Rebecca, but I didn't do it because there are very few qualities I value more than loyalty. I was impressed by her steadfastness, and I was moved by her dedication. Rebecca is now doing a great job for CNBC.

The most important thing to have in an office is team spirit, where each worker is committed to one another's success and to the success of the whole company. A group of solo players just out for their own glory does not work. Some of my best people have been with me for decades. I reward people highly for their loyalty to me and to the entire Trump Organization. We are all working together to become more successful.

My best employees have shown over the years that they will always be dedicated to what we are trying to accomplish. I reward them for that. I think the reason we have so many loyal people is that we reward loyalty, and everybody knows this. It has become part of the corporate culture of The Trump Organization. People like Allen Weisselberg and Matt Calamari are great and have proven themselves over many years.

Not every company is like this. A lot of companies demand loyalty from employees, but do not reciprocate. That is a sure way to lose good, talented people. The senior managers of The Trump Organization show as much loyalty to our employees as they show us, which is part of why we are so successful at keeping good people.

EVERYONE DESERVES A SECOND CHANCE

Recently, Miss USA, Tara Conner, broke pageant rules by using drugs and alcohol in excess publicly in New York City. I do not tolerate or condone that kind of out-of-control behavior in someone representing Miss USA. I do believe in giving second chances. I set up a meeting with her, and I had every intention of stripping her of her title. After talking to her, I realized the right thing to do in her case was to pardon her and give her a second chance. As you may know, this decision caused a media frenzy.

The media was very stirred up and demanded an explanation. I explained that Tara had made some bad decisions while she was on her own for the first time in New York City. She got too involved in the party scene and could not establish her own boundaries. Now she knows better. She is basically a good person who made a mistake. She is willing to learn from her mistake and to not let it happen again. Due to her willingness to change, I decided it was better to give her a second chance than to destroy her career and ruin her chances in life.

I believe giving Tara another chance was the right thing to do for many reasons. She worked hard to get that title. She made a mistake, but was determined not to do it again and to get the help she needed. She finished her reign and continues to support the goals of Miss USA completely.

Everyone in The Trump Organization knows that I forgave Tara, and they think it is great and it has solidified their allegiance to me. In return, I enjoy the freedom to make an occasional mistake myself because I have not set myself up to be perfect.

It is important to set this precedent. Everyone makes mistakes; all of us. Do not jump down the throat of every employee who makes a mistake. If you punish every mistake severely, you set a standard that is hard to achieve. Many people will play it too safe in order to not make mistakes. Mistakes will decrease, but so will productivity and ingenuity. If you want extraordinary results, you have to give people enough space to maneuver. You have to learn from mistakes, and you have to forgive and forget sometimes.

There are many times when it is not a good idea to forgive. I cannot and will not forgive people who have stolen, cooked the books, or engaged in fraud. I never forgive someone who makes bad decisions time and time again.

One characteristic I try to cultivate in employees is a concern for the organization as a whole. I reward employees who work wholeheartedly to bring more success to The Trump Organization as if the company's success were their own success. I respect employees who act quickly and can think on their feet. Time is often of the essence and I value staff members who are ready with answers and solutions.

I also like employees who save the company money. Companies suffer when employees do not make enough of an effort to control costs.

Finally, although some amount of personal ambition is necessary, too much could undermine the common goal of the company. The company has to come first in every employee's eyes. I always forgive honest mistakes and give good people second chances. Nobody always gets it right on the first try. Learn to forgive.

SET HIGH STANDARDS FOR YOURSELF AND EVERYONE ELSE

Expect the best from people. Very often they will rise to the challenge, and it is important to instill in them confidence to go along with the challenge. Give people the opportunity to excel. Without that opportunity, how will they shine? Also, do not limit their abilities according to their positions or titles. I have found many talented people who have potential that far exceeds their job title.

When I hired Matthew Calamari as a security guard more than twenty years ago, it became clear to me that he had a lot more to offer than his job title warranted. He went on to become an executive vice president, and is now the chief operating officer of Trump Properties. He has been a dedicated and trustworthy worker and, had he not been given challenges or responsibilities, this side of him would not have been apparent.

People should not be underestimated. Give them a chance; be the catalyst for their success. That way, everyone wins. Remember, you are not living in an ideal world. People are not perfect and some of them are outright vicious and hell-bent on doing you in. Use your gut to hire the best people you can find, but do not trust them. Create a work environment where you reward good people for doing good work and for being loyal to you and your company. Be demanding of people and they will rise to the occasion. Do not be too hard when they make mistakes; everyone makes mistakes. Always be willing to give someone who wants to do better a second chance.

ZANKER'S TAKE

You can only do so much yourself. You need other people to help you accomplish really big things in life. Hiring the best people can mean the difference between success and failure in business. Donald is right; you have to be on your guard to make sure that you avoid the worst in people and bring out the best. Here are some tips for managing people that have worked extremely well for me:

Sometimes Tip Before, not After

My pal John Goodfriend taught me "Tip the bartender generously when you have your first drink at a bar, not when you leave." I follow that rule both in my personal life and at work. My family once vacationed with another family at an "all inclusive" family resort in Jamaica. Both families had young kids, and we were thrilled that "all inclusive" included a nanny assigned to each family— all day, every day. I generously tipped our nanny as soon as we arrived, and she took great care of our kids and was enthusiastic and fun.

The other family went the traditional route: they tipped their nanny when they were checking out. Their nanny spent the week going through the motions—she was no fun at all. It did not matter that they were generous in the end; it was too late for their generosity to have any impact.

When I decided that The Learning Annex was going to launch a series of Wealth Expos, and I knew that my team was going to have to give 10,000 percent over the next year, I held an all-weekend staff meeting at the beautiful Doral Hotel in Westchester, NY, and the first thing I did to start the meeting was give out envelopes with $10,000 bonuses to everyone who was there. I told my team, "This is just a taste of the riches about to come your way." We held the most productive weekend planning meeting in Learning Annex history.

Staff who were away from their families called home and told their husbands and wives about their bonuses. So, instead of spouses complaining and my staff feeling guilty, the spouses were telling my staff, "Work hard this weekend. I will hold down the home front." For some of the people in the room, $10,000 was 25 percent of their salary. No one had expected it, and it changed the team's outlook. Now whenever the team goes away for a weekend retreat, everyone expects an envelope. And I never disappoint, since they deserve it.

Make Learning Fun

After our first expo, even though we made money, I insisted that the team meet and figure out how to make the next expo even better. One of the things we realized was that the weekend was too serious. People spent the whole weekend learning, but one of the hallmarks of The Learning Annex had always been that learning should be fun. How could we make it fun? Someone joked, "Hire ambassadors of fun." I heard that and said, "That's a great idea."

For the next expo in Los Angeles, I went out there a week early and went to bars, restaurants, taverns, and found the most cheerful, fun people, and hired them on the spot. I hired one hundred fun women and men. We sent them out into the crowd to give out candy and prizes, to cheer, dance, and throw beach balls. And it worked. The energy level was much higher, and everyone had more fun. Now we hire beautiful men and women who are totally choreographed "ambassadors of fun" performers for every expo we do, and many of them tour with us around the country.

I added some sex appeal to adult education in New York, and ultimately around the country, by putting good-looking women on the covers of our magazines, like other urban magazines such as *New York* magazine, *People, Us Weekly,* and *Esquire.* I took the staid industry of continuing education and made it sexy and fun. The same can be done for any business or industry. Look at a business with a different set of eyes. How can you change it, improve it, make it more user friendly?

Getting Advice from Experts

When you want advice from an expert, ask your question and sit quietly. Do not do what most people do and start to answer the question or make it multiple choice. You will only distract the expert, who will often just parrot back what he or she thinks you want to hear. If you truly want objective advice, do not be so insecure that you have to tell the expert how smart you are by suggesting answers. The expert is smart, and the expert is being paid. To get the best advice, let the expert work to find an answer based on his or her own experience and perspective.

Follow Jim Collins's advice from his excellent book *Good to Great: Why Some Companies Make the Leap . . . and Others Don't* and "put smart people on your bus."

When I first started The Learning Annex in the 1980s, it began growing so fast that I needed a chief financial officer right away. I could not find the right person. I took out ads, I asked around, and I even hired a headhunter who cost a bundle and sent me all the wrong people. Then I was having breakfast in a bagel shop in Greenwich Village one morning, and I noticed that the waiter looked familiar. I realized it was Clive Kabatznik, a guy I knew in college, and who I remembered as being very smart. I could not understand why such a smart guy was working in a bagel shop.

So we started to talk and get re-acquainted. He was originally from South Africa. He was touring around the United States and started working at the bagel store when he ran out of money. I soon discovered that he was basically open to anything. The only job opening I had was CFO. I thought, "He's smart. I trust him. What do I have to lose?" Clive turned into a great CFO and years after he left The Learning Annex, I still get great advice from him. He became a very successful entrepreneur having made millions starting and selling many companies. I always look first for smart people.

When I bought back The Learning Annex in 2001, I thought about who were the smartest people I knew and trusted, and how could I get them to work for me. My oldest friend Andy Hyams was one of the smartest people I knew. We had been best friends since fourth grade. Andy had gone to Harvard Law School and Harvard School of Public Health, and he had made a successful career in the public sector. I had always had great respect for the contributions he was making, but at the same time I got the sense that he was no longer being challenged. The way he talked about his work; his heart was not in it anymore.

I wanted him to work for The Learning Annex, but I did not want to pressure him. Then I saw my opportunity. I told Andy, "I'm treating you to a Tony Robbins Unleash the Power Within weekend," which is a three-day event where participants walk barefoot over several yards of hot coals. I had some doubt that Andy would go through with the fire walking part of the weekend, but Tony Robbins had plenty to offer even without the fire walking.

Andy was a big skeptic, and he gave me some great excuses for not going to the Tony Robbins weekend. But in the end he trusted me and went.

At the end of the weekend, he called me from San Diego. "Life changing," he said. "Really?" I was genuinely happy for him at that point. Nothing else really mattered. But I couldn't resist asking, "Did you do the fire walk?" He replied, "Yes. When I get back to work, I'm giving notice and I'm going to hang up a shingle. I am going to open my own law firm." I said, "Great. I'd be proud to be your first client."

People told me I was crazy for hiring a lawyer with zero experience in business, contracts, corporations, and tax law. I said, "Don't worry. First, he is smart, he has great judgment, and he isn't full of himself. Second, when he doesn't know something, chances are he can learn it. Third, if he can't learn it, I trust him to hire experts for us because he'll be as careful with The Learning Annex's money as he is with his own."

It all proved to be true. Andy has worked smartly and hard, and it has been great to have him join me on The Learning Annex's wave of success.

Like Donald Trump says, "Value loyalty above all else."

I am a little unorthodox when it comes to hiring, and, to be honest, most people that work with me do not last very long. The reason is that my standards are very high. As an entrepreneur I have learned that you have to lead by example. That is easy for me to do because I set high standards for myself. I work very long days, and I expect the same from my executives. I work weekends and holidays, and I expect the same of my team. If somebody wants a nine-to-five job, there is nothing wrong with that, but they are not going to succeed with me.

If a job applicant asks me what the hours are, the interview is over. It's not unusual for me to be emailing ideas back and forth with my executives at 2 A.M. To work these round-the-clock hours you need more than a good work ethic; you need passion for what you do and a hunger to do it better than any-body else. I am a risk taker and I like to hire risk takers.

For example, in 1986 a young kid approached me for a job. I kept turning him down since he had no experience. But he kept sending letters and stopping by the office. After six months of rejecting him, he offered to work for free. That was a crazy offer, but it showed me that he was hungry. He wanted to get his foot in the door at any cost. So I hired him. Harry Javer has been with me for twenty years and runs our mega expos and our operations.

Another great person on my team is Heather Moore. Heather had experience running night clubs and managing talent. She knew nothing about buying media. But she was conscientious, really cared, and had the "I can do anything attitude." Today Heather runs our media division, buying in excess of $20 million a year. She also runs our publishing department and public relations.

No one has titles on their business cards, mainly because at different meetings we all have different roles.

There are a handful of other employees and advisers that I have worked with through the years and they all share the same traits. They are passionate, loyal, diligent, and they all share my "sky is the limit" mentality. There is a saying: mediocrity stands in the way of greatness, and I try to think about that when I hire people. If they do not have the capacity to be great, they are just taking up space. If they cannot excel, then they are taking up the space of somebody who can.

Entrepreneurs do not have the luxury of enormous budgets and huge staffs; they have to hire people who can do the work of ten people. For this reason I tend to hire people who are smart, flexible, and generalists. When I need a specialist, I hire a consultant. If you hire smart people who are willing to work hard, you do not need a huge, expensive staff.

Share the wealth.

One more thing . . . I am a big believer that you have to reward people for the job they do. People that last with me get rewarded very well. We are in the expo business, but we function like a Wall Street firm: everybody shares in the wealth. I use this strategy with employees, consultants, and anybody I do business with. You have to give the people that work for you a piece of the pie. It is okay to overpay for people who deserve it. And if somebody is not pulling their weight, do not hesitate to get rid of them immediately before they spread the disease throughout your company—the disease of mediocrity.

I had an employee four years ago who was a booker . . . he booked our speakers. He was just okay. I took him out to lunch for a review and saw he was having trouble making ends meet. New York is an expensive city and since he had good taste in clothing and shoes, he was barely getting by. He was spending his time thinking about his money problems, and not about getting speakers. I didn't know what to do as we walked back from lunch to our offices. On Fifth Avenue he spotted a Versace suit in the window. He said, "That is an amazing suit." I said, "Let's go in and take a look." He tried on the suit and it was amazing . . . and so was the price tag. Around 7,000 dollars.

At the time I wanted to book Dr. Nicholas Perricone, the famous skin doctor, for a speaking tour of my cities. I knew he had been working for weeks to get the booking, but Perricone had proved to be very elusive. So I said,

"Get Perricone and I will buy you the suit." We got back to the office, and a few hours later, I saw he was leaving. I asked him, "Where are you going?" He said, "To pick up my suit." I looked at our big "bookings" whiteboard and sure enough he had nabbed Perricone. Business owners have to realize—if you want an outrageously great performance from an employee you have got to provide an outrageously great reward. He no longer works for me but before he left he thanked me for motivating him to outdo himself. It is a simple formula, but so many business owners cheap out and by doing that they only hurt themselves and their businesses. If an employee of mine works his guts out and as a result adds $100,000 to my bottom line, the $25,000 bonus is a bargain!

TO SUM IT UP

The world is a horrible place. Lions kill for food, but people kill for sport. People try to kill you mentally, especially if you are on top. We all have friends who want everything we have. They want our money, our business, house, car, wife, and dog. Those are our friends. Our enemies are even worse! You have got to protect yourself in life.

The same burning greed that makes people loot, kill, and steal in emergencies like fires and floods, operates daily in normal everyday people. It lurks right beneath the surface, and when you least expect it, it rears its nasty head and bites you. Accept it. The world is a brutal place. People will annihilate you just for the fun of it or to show off to their friends. Always hope for the best in people, but be prepared for the worst.

Take off the rose-colored glasses. Be paranoid. Be very careful when you hire people. If you do not watch your back, they will surely rip you off. Do not worry about being liked. It does not matter if your employees like you or not. Be damned sure that they respect you. I used to say, "Hire the best people and trust them." Now I know better. Now I say, "Hire the best people, and don't trust them."

KEY POINTS

▶ Do not have illusions; the world is a brutal place full of vicious people.

▶ Everyone wants to kill the fastest gun.

▶ Lions kill for food, humans kill for sport.

▶ Get some respect, and do not give a damn if people like you.

▶ Know your stuff and you will command instant respect.

▶ Always dress for respect.

▶ Get the best people, and do not trust them.

▶ Only hire people with positive attitudes and get rid of the "bad apples" fast.

▶ Inspire people with a powerful team spirit.

▶ Value loyalty above everything else.

▶ Forgive people for their first honest mistake.

▶ Never forgive a crook.

▶ Set high standards for people and expect they will fulfill them.

REVENGE

always get even. In the 1980s I recruited a woman from her job in government where she was making peanuts. She had nothing when she met me. I thought she was smart and that under my mentoring she could be very good. She was a nobody in her government job and going nowhere. I decided to make her into somebody. I gave her a great job at The Trump Organization, and over time she became powerful in real estate. She bought a beautiful home.

When I was going through tough times in the early 1990s, I needed her help. I asked her to make a phone call to an extremely close friend of hers who held a powerful position at a big bank and who would have done what she asked. She said, "Donald, I can't do that." I had taken her out of a dead-end government job. I encouraged her. I mentored her. I made her, and then she told me she couldn't do it. I got rid of her and then she started a business on her own.

Later I found out her business failed. I was really happy

DONALD J. TRUMP AND BILL ZANKER

when I found that out. She had turned on me after I had done so much to help her. I had asked for one favor in return, and she turned me down flat. She ended up losing her home. Her husband, who was only in it for the money, walked out on her, and I was glad. Over the years many people have called asking for a recommendation for her. I only give her bad recommendations. I just can't stomach the disloyalty.

I put the people who are loyal to me on a high pedestal and take care of them very well. I go out of my way for the people who were loyal to me in bad times. This woman was very disloyal, and now I go out of my way to make her life miserable. She calls asking to get together for lunch or for dinner. I never return her calls.

Over the years I have made many people successful. Some are thankful for it and some are not. Some have long memories and remember what you've done for them, even though they are no longer associated with you, but I find that most people forget.

One interesting story that took place recently was about a young golf pro, who was and is a fine player, but unable to get on the tour. He played the Nationwide Tour for a number of years, ultimately achieving PGA tour status. His first few months on the PGA tour he did very well, although since then, he has not done well at all.

180

Prior to his making any substantial money, I would let him practice and play at my highly rated course in Palm Beach, Florida, called Trump International Golf Club. For three years he would play the course, hit balls, practice, and thought of it as virtually his home course.

When he arrived on the tour and made a name for himself, my head golf pro at Trump International, John Nieporte, asked me if it would be all right, based on all we had done for him, to ask him to wear the Trump logo to various PGA tournaments. It wasn't exactly the most important thing in my life, but I said to John, "Sure, ask him, I'm sure he'll have no problem with that after all we did for him."

When John spoke to him, he said, "I'm sorry, John, I'll have to speak to my agent." So now I have instructed John, who was very surprised and in fact shocked at this, that after he is no longer on the tour, when he shows up for another round of golf, and wants to play the course, just respond by saying, "I'm sorry, but we'll have to call Mr. Trump's agent for permission."

Martha Stewart is another example. I was a good and loyal friend of hers. I helped her out after she got out of prison by promoting her TV show *The Apprentice: Martha Stewart.*

I was not a big fan of her show to begin with because I did not like the underlying idea—two versions of the same show. I thought it caused confusion. Still, NBC really wanted to try it.

The Apprentice was doing so well, they figured, "Hey, let's do another one."

The fact is Martha, instead of taking responsibility for the failure of her show, blamed it on me. I did nothing but promote Martha. I said she was a brave woman and she was working hard. I did not see the show until it aired. When I looked at the show, however, I realized it was never going to make it and she was terrible!

Martha told everybody her show was supposed to be the only *Apprentice* and that I had agreed to be fired by her on the air. That's just stupid. What moron would believe she was going to fire the guy with one of the top shows on television? The fact is her show did not work. For some reason Martha was not very good at it. She tried; she put in the effort, but she did not have what it took to make a successful show. In life, you have failures, and there is really nothing wrong with that, but when you have a failure, try not to blame other people. Martha's version of *The Apprentice* was a failure. Mine got great ratings. One worked—one did not.

What I am really most upset with Martha about, though, is her ingratitude. I was her single biggest promoter. I promoted her on every show, and I said what a wonderful woman she is, and I still believe that. Never once did she thank me. Never once did she call and say, "Donald, thank you very much." I defended Martha many, many times and I never got a note. I never got a phone call. One thing about life: when someone helps you, it's always nice to say thanks. I got tired of her attitude.

Then, when her show failed, she blamed me on top of everything else, but rather than play dead, I went on the attack. I wrote a scathing letter telling her that she had only herself to blame for her tanked show. I wrote, "Your performance was terrible. The show lacked mood, temperament and just about everything a show needs for success." I added, "I knew it would fail as soon as I first saw it—and your low ratings bore me out." My motto is: Always get even. When somebody screws you, screw them back in spades.

Sir Richard Branson and Mark Cuban also failed with their poor copies of *The Apprentice*. Richard Branson, who owns Virgin Atlantic Airways, is a good guy. He called me recently, but I have to tell you this story.

Last year I was upset with him because he was doing a new show, a copy of *The Apprentice,* named *The Rebel Billionaire: Branson's Quest for the Best*. Nobody ever remembers the name of his show. Two months before the show was going to air he started promoting it with hot air balloons and media hype. They call him a billionaire, but how can anyone become a billionaire owning an airline? The fact is, he has other good businesses but airplanes are expensive, there is too much competition, and ticket prices are too low to make a profit. I don't know how anyone could become a billionaire running an airline. Maybe that's why he wanted to do a reality show. Anyway, before the show went on the air, they interviewed him on Fox, asking him what he thought of Donald Trump. He is my friend, so he said, "Oh, he's great. Donald is a friend of mine. He's a great businessman and very successful. I respect him a lot."

Then about two weeks before the show, some moron producer told Branson, "You can't say nice things about Trump. You have to say horrible things about Trump." Richard said, "Why?" The producer said, "Because you have to say outrageous things about him to get good ratings." Then, a week before the show went on the air, he said, "I don't like Donald Trump and he doesn't like shaking peoples' hands." He had lots of bad things to say about me.

It was bad enough that he was trying to knock off my show, now he was insulting me on top of it. I vowed to get revenge. I didn't say anything about it then. I waited until his show went on the air. I did not want to attack him if the show became a big success. I didn't want to look foolish. Frankly, I did not want to help his ratings by giving him publicity.

Finally it went on the air, and it tanked, only getting 4.85 million viewers. The critics hated it. *The Washington Post* TV critic Tom Shales called it silly, stupid and ridiculous. The network quickly cancelled the show, because it was so bad. Now it was my moment. I went after that guy like crazy. I told the *New York Daily News,* "I thought the show was terrible. *The Apprentice* is the hottest show there is! Richard Branson, your ratings speak very loudly, and you just got fired!"

When Cuban's show failed, I wrote a letter to the *New York Post* stating that I could have saved him a lot of time and energy in that I understand life, business, and television. Mark Cuban has absolutely zero television persona or personality. He's got the look of a Neanderthal, and he just doesn't get it. Most importantly, he is not a winner. When his team should have won the NBA playoffs the season before last, they totally choked in the stretch and lost to the Miami Heat and the great Shaquille O'Neal, a friend of mine, and Dwayne Wade. This year was even worse. They went into the playoffs, predicted to win the NBA championship, and instead lost in the first round to a totally unheralded Golden State Warriors team.

When Mark did his show on ABC called *The Benefactor,* it was an immediate and resounding failure—it drew flies and was thrown off the air very quickly. In order to get a little buzz and excitement, he said things about me that weren't true. He stated that he was at my Mar-a-Lago house many years ago and I called him over and belittled people that were not on my economic level. That's not my deal—in fact, my deal is the exact opposite. I have much more fun belittling people like Mark Cuban. Besides, I don't like people that make up stories! I have always said that Mark Cuban is a loser—time will prove me right. Branson, on the other hand, is a good guy.

WHEN SOMEBODY HITS YOU, HIT 'EM BACK HARDER

With Rosie O'Donnell it got a lot worse. Rosie O'Donnell is a total degenerate. She attacked Kelly Ripa, who's a wonderful person, because Clay Aiken put his hand over her mouth to shut her up. Rosie attacked Kelly for that incident. Kelly's nice, and she didn't really attack Rosie back. Rosie attacked Danny DeVito. She talked about him as if he was an alcoholic because he went out drinking with George Clooney the night before a show. He's not an alcoholic. I know him; he is a friend of mine. I called him, and I said, "Danny, she called you an alcoholic. Why don't you do something about it?" This is before I had a problem with her. I told him, "Go on television and announce that she's bad news, and you're not an alcoholic." He said, "Ah, I don't want to get involved." I said, "All right, you've got a different personality than I do!"

One day I got a call from a newspaper reporter telling me that "Rosie went on this ranting, raving lunatic tirade about you for about ten minutes on *The View*." Basically, she attacked me, because I gave Tara Conner, the then current Miss USA, a second chance when everybody thought I was going to fire her. She insulted me in many ways and said some very ugly things about me.

Tara Conner is a very lovely young lady. But she had some problems adjusting to the pressures of New York City. She started doing drugs and alcohol. It was causing lots of difficulties. But after talking with Tara, I decided to give her a second chance. She agreed to go to rehab and is now doing fine. She thanked me for "saving her life."

Rosie O'Donnell, however, did not like that I gave Tara a second chance. She went on television and the venom came pouring out. A friend of mine called and said, "Boy, does she hate you." I have known Rosie for a long time. She has always been bad news.

She was fired from her television show, *The Rosie O'Donnell Show*, because of bad ratings. She made a total disaster of her magazine. Her meddling and viciousness destroyed the morale of everyone that worked for her magazine. The publisher of the company, who was a rising star, ended up losing his job. Her Broadway play was a total mess. She is an unattractive person both inside and out. Rosie is about as low as you can go. She is a bully who has been that way for a long time.

Now I had a choice; I could attack back, or I could let it pass. I chose to attack her so hard she would rue the day she decided to attack me. The media was very interested in my response. I gave them an earful! I got calls from *Entertainment Tonight, Inside Edition, Access Hollywood, Extra,* and others asking, "Do you have a response?" Yes, I had a response. I said, "Rosie O'Donnell is disgusting, both inside and out. Take a look at her, she's a slob. She talks like a truck driver, her show failed, her magazine was a total catastrophe, she got sued. So, I'll probably sue her, because it would be fun. I'd like to take some money out of her pockets." I said, "Rosie is a very unattractive woman who is a bully. Rosie is a loser and ultimately *The View* will fail because of Rosie. Barbara Walters made a mistake in hiring her." And Barbara told me, "Donald, don't get into the mud with pigs."

One morning I went on *The Today Show* to talk about *The Apprentice,* but instead Meredith Vieira started asking me questions about Rosie. Right off she asked me, "Donald, why did you attack Rosie?" What nerve! Rosie attacked me. I was just fighting back. Then she asked, "Is it true that you said she was crude?" I said, "No, I never said that, it's not strong enough, I said, 'She's a total degenerate!'" Then she asked, "Is it true that you called her a fat pig?" I said, "No, I called her a pig!"

It is funny; I called her a total degenerate, and nobody cared, but when they thought I called her "fat" they were all going ballistic! Rosie said her children came up to her and said, "Mommy, Mommy, he called you the F-word." I don't believe her children ever said that.

I replied to Meredith, "I didn't say she was fat, because that's politically incorrect. Come to think of it, Meredith, is she fat?" Meredith evaded the question with "Well I'd rather not answer that." I pressed the point. "Meredith, I want to know, is she fat?" She sidesteps again with, "I don't think I should answer that!" Then I said, "Assuming I did call her a fat pig, do you think I'd be wrong? I didn't, but do you think I'd be wrong?" Then she said, "Let's get off this subject."

That just shows you that these TV reporters really have no guts. I mean, I love Meredith; she's very nice, but she did the wrong thing. Then she came back with another stupid question, "Donald, why do you always talk about Rosie?" I said, "Because you asked me questions!" I didn't bring Rosie up. It was the dumbest interview I think I've ever had in my life.

About that time, Rosie announced that she suffers from depression. Reporters called me for a comment. Rather than saying, "I have no comment." Or, as most people would say, "Isn't that too bad? Oh, that's so bad." I said, "I think I can cure her depression. If she'd stop looking in the mirror I think she'd stop being so depressed." That went on *Entertainment Tonight*, and the reporter said, "Oh, it was a horrible statement. It was horrible." What is so horrible about it? She attacks me and tells ugly lies about me, but I am not allowed to attack back?

Here's the point: a few days later Rosie is interviewed on the red carpet. The reporter asked, "Rosie, Donald said you shouldn't look in a mirror, it will solve your problems with depression. Do you have a comment?" She replied, "I have no comment. I don't want to talk about him!" You know why? Because I hit that horrible woman right smack in the middle of the eyes. It's true. She'll talk about Kelly Ripa, she'll talk about Danny DeVito, or Tom Selleck, but, you know, when you hit a bully back they always fold. I learned it in high school, you've got to hit a bully really hard, really strongly, right between the eyes. Some people would have ignored her insults. I decided to fight back and make her regret the day she decided to unload on me!

That is why I tell people, "Get even!" This is not your typical advice, get even, but this is real-life advice. If you don't get even, you are just a schmuck! I really mean it, too. For some reason, athletes like me and they call me a lot. I know many athletes that have lost a tremendous amount of money. They are young kids who make a lot of money at a very young age, and they lose most of it before they retire. They have nothing left. It is all gone, because they have managers, accountants, lawyers, agents, and so called financial advisers that take it away. To them it is like taking candy from a baby.

An athlete friend of mine called me one day and told me he had evidence that his manager had stolen all his money. He is a great athlete who played for years in the NBA. He said, "Mr. Trump, with the information I found, I have this guy cold, right?" This athlete is very famous, and you all know his name, even if you're not a big fan. I said, "Let's go get that mother you know what! Let's go get him! I can help you get him. I've got the nastiest lawyer that you could imagine. We're going to sue your manager's ass off. We're going to hurt him so badly he's going to come back to you on his knees." I added, "I'm going to go get this guy for you and he's going to suffer and you are going to get a lot of your money back, whatever this guy hasn't squandered." Then he said, "Oh, Mr. Trump, don't do it, I don't want to do that." I said, "What do you mean, you don't want to do it? Why?" He said, "Well, I don't want to get involved." I said, "Why?"

Here is a great athlete who lost all his money, and yet he does not want to get involved in going after his manager who robbed him blind. He did not steal nice and easy or make a little mistake, he robbed him. I said, "Listen, you have to do this, or you're the dumbest person I've met in a long time!" He said, "I can't do it!" I said, "That's okay, but never, ever call me again, because you are a schmuck!" I have not spoken to the guy since. He calls me once in a while, but I don't ever talk to him, because he is a loser. You have to show people you can't be pushed around. His next manager, whoever it may be—and he does not have long to go in his career—will probably steal the money he is making now. Why shouldn't he? This guy is not going to go after him, because he is a jerk.

So do not hesitate to go after people. This is important not only for the person you are going after but for other people to know not to mess around with you.

When other people see that you don't take crap and see you are really going after somebody for wronging you, they will respect you. Always have a good reason to go after someone. Do not do it without a good reason. When you are wronged, go after those people because it is a good feeling and because other people will see you doing it.

Getting even is not always a personal thing. It's just a part of doing business. An example is my dealings with Merv Griffin. Merv Griffin recently passed away—he was an interesting character. He and I fought quite a bit, but in the end I think we gained a mutual respect. He would tell people that Donald Trump was a genius (I think he even wrote it in his book), but one thing never changed—Merv would state to everybody that he beat me in a deal when in actuality he knew better and admitted such to me.

I sold him a company called Resorts International for a very high price. I had most of the voting stock so there was nothing he could have done unless I was willing to sell, but his price was so high that it would have been insane not to take his offer. Immediately after the deal was made, Merv went around telling everybody that he beat me. "I beat Donald Trump at the deal!" he would shout.

Newspapers and magazines were calling me and exclaiming that Merv beat Donald in a deal. I'll never forget telling one of the reporters, "Deals are funny—tell me about it in five years, but in the meantime I got a very high price, much more than he would have had to pay, because I would have taken far less."

In any event the deal turned out to be a disaster for Merv, and to the best of my knowledge he filed for Chapter 11 on this transaction at least two times. I believe that is why he called me a genius, but I can also say he was an amazing competitor; very nice and smooth on the outside but a real tiger from within. He did say, at a certain event, "I used to have a lot of coconuts," jokingly referring to how much the Resorts International deal with me cost him. Because of business Merv and I were not friends—but I will miss him.

I love getting even when I get screwed by someone—yes, it is true, people still try to take me for a ride, and sometimes they succeed, rarely, but when they do I go after them. You know what? People do not want to play around with me as much as they do with others. They know if they do, they are really in for a big fight. Always get even. When you are in business you need to get even with people who screw you. You need to screw them back fifteen times harder. You do it not only to get the person who messed with you but also to show the others who are watching what will happen to them if they mess with you. If someone attacks you, do not hesitate. Go for the jugular. Attack them back in spades!

ZANKER'S TAKE

Life is full of losers who love to mess with people, especially people who are successful. I think it comes down to one of two things: jealousy or greed, or a combination of the two. Sometimes there is no money involved, as Donald says, "They just do it for sport."

One time a company came out with a complete knockoff of The Learning Annex and started promoting it in direct competition with me in New York City. They were basically stealing our customers. I sent a letter asking the owner to stop ripping us off. They refused, so I immediately sued for copyright violations and trademark infringement. When we went to court, the judge asked them if they wanted to settle out of court. They said "no." So the judge ruled in The Learning Annex's favor and set the other company's fine so high that it could not pay it and had to go under. I felt very good about this. You have to go after people who mess with you.

Persistence is crucial. My whole company was at stake. I could not lie down and just take it. I had to fight back. I saw the fight all the way to the New York State Court of Appeals, the highest court in New York. I kept fighting until I won. Never stop until you get even.

Another time in the 1980s when my business was really getting off the ground, I hired a speaker who was a bestselling author and expert on relationships. She was scheduled to speak at The Learning Annex in Washington, D.C., on a Saturday morning. Her flight was due to arrive from Los Angeles on Friday night. We had hundreds of people signed up for her class.

At 11 P.M. she called to tell me that her flight had been cancelled and that she would not be able to teach the class. I was in a real bind because these people needed help and were looking forward to the class. It was too late to contact all those people and tell them that the event was cancelled. They would come to the class the next day, and find out that it was not going to happen. That was not a good thing for my business or my reputation.

I checked with the airlines and found out that the flight was not cancelled at all. It was clear to me that she had just decided at the last minute not to honor her commitment. She would rather disrespect me and all the people who had signed up for the class.

If she would have owned up to what she did and apologized for causing me problems, I would have let it go. But she treated me and the students who were attending the class like we didn't matter. After that happened, I started making a list of people that hurt me. I put her name on the list. Then I sat back and waited for a chance to get revenge. Sometimes my list is short, other times it grows. But I always have my list and trust me, you never want to be on my list.

Some time later a TV producer called me. This same author was being considered for a TV show about relationships. She gave my name as a reference. I gave this woman the worst possible recommendation you could imagine. I told them she was a terrible person, an extremely dishonest and irresponsible person.

Later I was happy to hear that she never got that show off the ground. I am not sure if my bad reference had something to do with it, but I certainly hope so. She has called many times to try to get booked for classes at The Learning Annex to promote her books, but I never let her speak. I never forgot how rude and disrespectful she acted toward me and my students. I never let things like that pass. I always get even.

Recently, I had to fire an employee for incompetence. I hate firing people. But this guy did a terrible job, and I had to let him go. A few weeks later I got a letter from an attorney stating that he was suing me for wrongful termination. There was completely no justification for this suit. But it would cost me a bundle to defend. So I decided to get even instead.

I got an idea. I called my tech guy into my office and asked him to look through all the deleted files on the computer that this person had used while he worked for me, and to see what he had been up to while he was supposedly working for me. My computer expert came back with some interesting stuff. Apparently this guy had been surfing hundreds of porn sites from his work computer.

I had my lawyer send a letter to his lawyer explaining that if we were to go to court, all this information about him would be made public. (That I did not care one bit about all the scorn and embarrassment he would suffer.) I never heard from him again. It just shows that you have to play hardball when someone tries to bully you.

Always make a list of people who hurt you. Then sit back and wait for the appropriate time to get revenge. When they least expect it, go after them with a vengeance. Go for their jugular. Now, if you get a sincere apology from someone and if they owe you money and pay you, I accept it and let it go. But if not, just wait for the opportunity and when it comes, hit 'em hard.

TO SUM IT UP

As a child your parents and teachers told you not to fight and to try to get along with people. They meant well, trying to protect you from the harsh realities of the world, but in the world of grown-ups, things are different. Many bullies out there try to push you around. They can get very nasty. When a bully comes after you, do not fold up and play nice. Do not lie down and take it, "Get even!" This is not your typical advice, but it is real-life advice. If you do not get even you are just a schmuck! Most business writers won't be so blunt and honest with you about getting even. They know it's the truth, but won't tell you because they want people to think of them as a "nice person." I don't like to mince words. When you're wronged and you do nothing about it, you aren't "nice" you're a schmuck.

That's why I say when you are wronged, go after those people, because it is a good feeling, and because other people will see you doing it. I love it. Because I get screwed all the time, so I go after people. You know what, people don't want to mess with me as much as others. They know if they do they are really in for a big fight. Always get even.

KEY POINTS

- ▶ When somebody screws you, screw them back in spades.

- ▶ Forgive good people, but never forgive someone who is bad.

- ▶ When someone attacks you publicly, always strike back.

- ▶ If you want to stop a bully, hit them right between the eyes. They will think twice about doing it again.

- ▶ Even some of the toughest top athletes are schmucks who let people steal from them and are afraid to get even.

- ▶ Always have a good reason to get even.

- ▶ Go for the jugular so that people watching will not want to mess with you.

- ▶ If someone knows they made a mistake and they apologize, forgive them and move on, but never trust them again.

7

BIG MO!

t is very important to know when it is your time. I learned an important lesson in momentum and timing from William Levitt, the amazing father of suburbia. William Levitt became so famous that he made the cover of *Time* magazine on July 3, 1951. It all started after the end of World War II.

Prior to World War II there was no housing industry as we know it today; just local builders who could not build more than a few houses a year. That way of building was much too slow and cumbersome to keep up with the swelling demand for housing brought on by the millions of servicemen and women returning home after the war. People were so hard up for housing that one couple camped out for two days in a New York City department store window to publicize their plight.

William Levitt solved the post–World War II housing crisis by applying assembly-line techniques to housing construction. He was able to put up large numbers of houses quickly and cheaply. Levitt's houses were so cheap that bus drivers, teachers, and mill workers could afford them. He was a brilliant builder who created modern building methods and was responsible for the invention of modern suburbia as we know it today. He broke down the construction process into twenty-seven distinct operations and built houses using specialized teams for carpentry, tiling, painting, roofing, and so on.

Bill Levitt was very hungry. He was on top of every detail. When he was building 17,000 houses at a time in Levittown, New York, he would go himself, after a day of construction, to pick up nails. He would make sure his workers picked up sawdust, because they could make money selling it to other companies. He kept lumber costs down by buying his own forests and sawmills. He cut out the distributor markup by buying appliances directly from manufacturers. He even manufactured his own nails. Levitt insisted on perfection. Every Saturday he would drive his black Cadillac around the streets of Levittown, checking on the doings in the town he created. He listened for gossip and made sure everything was in tip-top condition.

Levitt built 140,000 modest, low- and middle-class homes all over the United States and Canada, including New York, Pennsylvania, New Jersey, Maryland, and Georgia. In 1968 Levitt sold his company to ITT, a big conglomerate run by Harold Geneen, who was a great businessman. Levitt received $92 million in stock, which is like $2 billion today.

Levitt retired and married a beautiful wife, some people would say a trophy wife. Then he proceeded to spend most of his money on luxuries like his 237-foot yacht, *La Belle Simone*, (named after his third wife) and a 30-room mansion in Mill Neck, New York. He lived very easily and peacefully. As part of the deal he made when he sold his company, he agreed not to build anything in the United States for ten years. However, he started some building projects in locations such as Iran, Venezuela, and Nigeria. He used his ITT stock as collateral for the loans he took out to build his new projects.

In the meantime, after ITT took over Levitt's housing business, ITT did not manage it as well as Levitt had. Instead of using ingenuity to solve problems, this huge conglomerate tried to solve problems by throwing a lot of money at them. ITT did not know what it was doing. It wasted a lot of money. It did not go around picking up nails. It did not care about the details. It recklessly squandered money by buying land in many different places before discovering that the land could not be zoned. ITT was doing all the things that a big company does, and was losing money, but it did not care. Within four years the ITT stock lost 90 percent of its value. When its foreign projects got into financial trouble the company was left with millions of dollars in debt.

After fifteen years ITT decided to put Levitt's company up

for sale. Levitt, wanting back into the action, bought his own company back from ITT. Levitt started building houses in the United States again, but he never regained his previous glory; he ran into a tough recession and many other problems that he could not solve. He ended up going bankrupt and losing everything.

In 1993 I was invited to a party for 100 ultra-successful people hosted by a powerful businessman in his Fifth Avenue apartment. After my troubles of the early 1990s had subsided, I was starting to do really well: I had purchased 40 Wall Street and was building Trump International Hotel and Tower, and I was invited to the party, even though I do not drink. At the party, an old man was sitting in the corner. I walked up to talk to him and realized it was William Levitt, the great home builder. He was about eighty-two years old. Nobody else was even talking to him, because they were all talking among themselves and doing deals. I was shocked that he was there.

As a real estate person, I was very interested in talking to him, because I had always respected his work. I said, "Hi, Mr. Levitt, how are you doing?" He said, "Not well, Donald, not well at all." I said, "I know. I've been reading that things have been very tough for you." He said, "It's been very, very tough and very humiliating." I was curious, and I said, "What exactly went wrong?"

He said, "Donald, I lost my momentum." This is the same brilliant, dynamic man who built 140,000 homes and revolutionized the housing industry. The same man, only he had lost his momentum and lost everything. That is the only time I ever heard that statement made.

We are all capable of losing our momentum and if that time comes, you have to know what to do about it, because there is no reason to put yourself in that position. I thought his insight was so brilliant. It was so amazing and very sad. He died shortly thereafter with nothing, because he lost his momentum. I learned a great lesson from William Levitt that night. Since then, I have devoted a lot of time to studying and applying the power of momentum to my own life and business. I do not ever want to lose my momentum. The lesson applies whether you are in real estate or not.

When you start toward a worthy goal—like landing a great job on Wall Street or becoming the next mayor of New York or building the world's tallest building—you have not yet built any momentum. You have no contacts and no track record. Nobody is calling you and nothing is happening.

Momentum works like this—I will use real estate as an example, but the same thing applies to salespeople, politicians, entrepreneurs, inventors, company executives, lawyers, and just about every profession—first, you go out and beat your head against a wall looking for deals and properties, with no luck.

You keep on doing it and at the same time you go out and line up a team of professionals to call on once you have a building or renovation project: appraisers, surveyors, lawyers, accountants, and contractors. At first nobody knows you. They do not believe you because you have never done anything before. They can't tell if you are the real deal or just another fly-by-night operation that will fold up and move on when things get too tough. At first nothing is happening.

With each passing day and each contact you make, you are silently building momentum. You are showing people that you are not going away and still nothing happens. So you keep that up. Then one day, something breaks for you; you land an account or sign a deal. You tell all your contacts, and all of a sudden your credibility rises. They start to believe you. You keep on working, and now you are at a somewhat higher level. After a while you have so much momentum built up that things start to come to you in multiples: two or three jobs or clients or deals come your way all at once. You tell everybody about this, and your value goes up tremendously. Everybody sees that you have momentum, and they want to be a part of it!

What can you do to establish momentum? To get momentum, you must first focus on a specific goal with passion and intensity, as I have previously discussed. Pick something you are very good at or have the ability to become good at. Start your momentum rolling by becoming very knowledgeable about your chosen field.

When I was studying finance at Wharton, the standard courses were great, but they did not fully satisfy my thirst for real-world knowledge. I knew that I wanted to be a big real estate developer and so, in my spare time at Wharton, I studied how to buy and sell real estate. It was not part of the curriculum, but I studied it anyway, and I started creating some personal momentum.

Getting a good mentor helps create momentum, too. Find someone knowledgeable about your field, and make them your friend. Ask their advice. If you have a question about something you do not understand, ask your mentor. If you do not have a mentor that you can meet face-to-face, find a mentor through your studies or your reading. Find someone who appeals to you and has achieved something you admire and aspire toward. For example, if you are interested in architecture, study the careers and lives of great architects, past and present. It is important to give yourself a good foundation first. Many accomplished people will not have the time to devote to novices. Get as much technique and background knowledge as you can on your own.

To me, a good mentor is someone who gives opportunities as well as challenges as teaching tools. We all need to know our weak spots as well as our strengths. If you watch *The Apprentice*, you will notice that personal strengths and weaknesses are often made apparent by the candidates themselves, without me having to point them out. Challenge yourself, critique yourself and keep moving forward to gain confidence and stamina.

My mentor was my father. When I graduated from Wharton, I started putting that knowledge to work in the real world by working for my father on real estate deals, which boosted my momentum significantly. To build momentum, get a job in your field as soon as you can. Work in the mailroom or as a summer intern—whatever you need to do to get your foot in the door and start to establish real-world momentum.

It was great working for my father, but I wanted more. A very important point is that to keep the momentum growing, you must continually challenge yourself. I challenged myself in a big way when I took the plunge and moved to Manhattan to start my own business. I took the momentum that I had carefully built while working for my father in Queens and Brooklyn for five years and used it to launch my real estate development career in the big-time arena of Manhattan. Then I used the focus of my will and the power of my enthusiasm to build even more momentum. Momentum is like poker chips that you have to keep in the game and keep putting into successively bigger and bigger pots.

There is a funny thing about momentum: when you stop, it stops. That is what happened to me in the late 1980s. I rode a wave of momentum to the top of New York's real estate world. I had done my preparatory work and the timing was perfect. I came on the scene exactly when real estate in New York City was at its low point. I got into the game when the undervalued, bargain-basement West Side Penn Central properties came on the market and nobody but me was interested in them. I got into that deal with no money. After that the real estate market in Manhattan took off on a sixteen-year boom. All I ever saw were the good times. I thought it would always be that way. Over those sixteen booming years I had always been intent on one thing: building bigger and bigger momentum. Then I stopped.

Business Week came out with a feature article about me that stated, "Everything he touches turns to gold." I believed that the article was true, and I started acting as if the article were true. I went to Paris and enjoyed myself with the other great love of my life: beautiful women—supermodels. I had lost track of reality. I thought real estate was easy. I never imagined that the momentum that had grown bigger and bigger with every deal would ever stop. That is exactly what happened, and it almost destroyed me. That is the other interesting truth about momentum: if you do not keep it growing, it will not just stand still; it will turn on you and take down everything you have built. That is what happened to Bill Levitt, and that is what almost happened to me.

WHAT DOES NOT KILL YOU MAKES YOU STRONGER

A setback can either (1) destroy you, or (2) make you stronger. There is an old saying that I believe, "Whatever doesn't kill you makes you stronger." I have the greatest respect for people who have experienced adversity and then come back. I was one of those people in the early 90s. I went through a tough period and learned a lot about myself, and then I came back bigger and better and stronger. It was not unlike what happened to Frank Sinatra in the early 50s. Like me, he lost focus. He took his eye off the ball and he made some bad decisions. (Also like me, it was beautiful women that had a little something to do with his troubles, but that is another story for another time.)

Sammy Davis Jr. tells a wonderful story in his book, *Yes I Can*, where Sammy, who is on the way up (due in no small part to Sinatra's patronage), sees Frank walking down Broadway all by himself, looking utterly dejected. At the time, Frank was on the skids, having gone from being the biggest singer ever known to a laughingstock, reduced to singing novelty songs.

This experience was a wake-up call for Frank. After that he regained his focus and his success.

I can tell a lot about a person by the way they handle difficult situations. I have seen many seemingly tough guys fold under pressure. I have noticed that it is a matter of how you define your setback or challenge: if you admit defeat, then you will be defeated. If you accept that the situation is bad, but you are determined to see it through, then you have a much better chance. It is your choice. It is frightening when bad things happen. I know that from personal experience. I did not let them destroy my confidence.

You never really know how bad a situation is going to be. You never know how it is going to turn out. I was in the worst situation imaginable, and when it was all over, it turned out great. I did not know at the time that it was going to end okay, but in my heart and my mind I defined it as a setback that I could overcome.

I had friends who chose to give up on themselves and declare their own defeat. What a stupid thing to do! Of course, they never made it through. Never declare yourself beaten. If you fail at something, it is okay. That may be out of your control, but never voluntarily throw in the towel. Always keep fighting! You never know when there is another chance or another great opportunity waiting right around the corner.

ROLL THE BOULDER UP THE HILL

I had lost my focus and suddenly I was faced with some major setbacks. The banks were out to get me in a big way. My momentum had come to a standstill. It was terrible but I did not quit; I kept moving forward while trying to learn from my mistakes. I stayed focused on my work, plans for new deals and new properties, because that is what made me feel good. Working on new projects helped me to regain my momentum slowly but surely and after a while things turned around for me in a big way.

What I learned from my setback is that you have to maintain your focus and keep building your momentum at all times. Your problems can be temporary if you keep your momentum moving forward. Again, it is all in how you look at things and how you define your situation. If you feel that all hope is lost, then it is. If you view a setback as a temporary lull or slowdown that will pick up again if you keep working at what you love, then that will be your reality.

We all experience difficulties. That is life. You show your true colors in how you handle devastating events. Time will heal all wounds, just remain positive and move on. Whenever I approach a project I know there will be problems. I expect them. I do not cry about them, because I know it is my job to solve them. Be the one to solve tough problems and you will be the one people pay big money for.

Anyone can do things that are easy. It is rare to find people who can tackle big challenges. If you do, you stand out from the crowd. I have found that if something is too easy, it is not usually even worth doing. Lots of other people are already doing it, and there usually is not much profit in the easy jobs. My business is so hard that sometimes I feel like Sisyphus, who was condemned to roll a boulder uphill for eternity.

That is just the way it is sometimes, so I just keep going; I don't give up. My focus is intense enough to make the effort worth it, and my momentum makes sure that my efforts will not be futile. I have learned a lot from demanding situations.

PLOUGH RIGHT THROUGH YOUR PROBLEMS

Mistakes happen every day, so expect them and learn to deal with them. Things do not always go as planned. You are not being a pessimist or a negative thinker by expecting mistakes; you are just being realistic and prepared to survive any challenge in life as a way to protect yourself. Problems, setbacks, mistakes, and losses are all a part of life. They are something you have to accept. Do not let yourself be shocked if and when they happen. Be prepared. The more prepared you are, the less likely it is that problems will knock you off balance.

If something unexpected takes you by surprise, keep your cool. Just say to yourself, "I should have known." Be flexible and adjust to the bad event without missing a beat. Later ask yourself how you could have prepared for the problem in advance. Learn as much as you can from the situation, then move on. It will be unlikely you will make the same mistake again. That is how to handle mistakes and problems. That is how to grow and become a master of your business, your career, and your life.

There is a time, however, in some endeavors, whether it is in a business, a career or a relationship, when it is time to call it quits. Sometimes things happen that make you question whether you should keep going. As long as you are enjoying what you are doing and are making progress, keep going. Do not let nagging doubts and insecurities stop you. Self-doubt is normal. If you are no longer passionate about your career anymore, then find something you are passionate about.

My motto is: "Never give up." I follow this very strictly. I only give up on something when it is perfectly clear that there is no other option. I do not let problems and challenges stop me; they are normal in any endeavor, but when dishonesty and outright cruelty creep into any undertaking, I closely re-evaluate my reasons for being involved.

In 1975, when I was working with the city and the banks to put together a deal that would save the area around Grand Central Terminal and 42nd Street from ruin, I had a very difficult time. The banks would not give me a loan without tax abatement from the city. The city would not give me tax abatement without a loan from a bank. Neither side would budge. I spent many long months of negotiating back and forth and proving to the city and the banks that this deal would work and that everybody was going to be happy with the Grand Hyatt Hotel that I was planning to build to replace the old Commodore Hotel.

Finally, the city agreed to give me a very generous tax abatement. When I told the news to the bank they still wanted to drag their feet on the financing. Then many of the big New York developers got wind of the huge tax abatement and protested. The project was one delay after another, and it really tested my resolve. When one re-negotiation after another failed, I felt like giving up. However, I refused to quit. I kept hammering away and finally closed the deal. It turned out to be a huge success, good for the city, the bank, and me.

That experience taught me to always expect setbacks, to solve them one by one and to never quit until the job is done.

You have to be the same way. Do not be afraid of mistakes and setbacks, because they are your best teachers. Learn from them. Use the knowledge to build something great for yourself.

WHEN YOU REACH THE TOP, GIVE BACK

One way to keep your momentum going is to keep giving yourself greater and greater challenges. Once you have reached the top, what do you do? Once you have reached the top, it is time to give back. Give to charity, give to your children, give your knowledge to others, and give to your culture. I made a lot of money, and I give a lot of money away to charity.

Warren Buffett is a great example: billionaire investor Warren Buffett is distributing more than $30 billion of his stock to the Bill and Melinda Gates Foundation, which focuses on global health issues such as the GAVI Alliance, which distributes vaccines to children in poor countries and to education such as the United Negro College Fund's Gates Millennium Scholars Program. Buffett wants his money to be used to tackle some of the complex problems that are the most difficult to solve. His children were 100 percent okay with that.

It is also important to give your knowledge and insight freely to anyone who asks. I believe people absorb more efficiently and faster when they learn by doing, and I am intent on giving people the knowledge they need to succeed. I give two-hour speeches at The Learning Annex Wealth Expos for the same purpose, and I donate a large portion of my speaking fees to charity.

To keep your momentum going you must have intrinsic values as well as monetary values, and you must recognize when it is time to start giving back.

ZANKER'S TAKE

I always go with my momentum. After the big front page newspaper stories in 1982 about The Learning Annex's attempt to drop $10,000 from the Empire State Building (see story in Chapter Four: *Creating Luck*), I used the momentum caused by that amazing bit of luck to propel the company higher. We also used the momentum of our speakers to drive our growth. We have gotten momentum from many speakers including Tony Robbins, George Foreman, Robert Kiyosaki, Jim Cramer, and many others. Our association with Donald Trump has put our company on the map and given us hyper-momentum. It was hold on and strap yourself to this rocket called Donald. It has been an incredible ride. Finding a partner to align yourself with can sure get momentum going.

Speaking of momentum, last year a little-known movie called *The Secret* swept onto the world stage to capture the attention of millions of Americans. It is still spreading across the world like wildfire. It is discussed on hundreds of forums and websites. Millions of enthusiastic fans are buying *The Secret* DVD and book of the same name and causing *The Secret* to rocket to the top of every major bestseller list.

Experts from *The Secret* have appeared on the *Oprah Winfrey Show, The Ellen DeGeneres Show, Larry King Live,* and *The Montel Williams Show.* The *Los Angeles Times* has proclaimed *The Secret* to be a "cultural phenomenon." In a nutshell, *The Secret* tells you how to use supercharged thoughts to propel yourself to success in business and in every aspect of your life.

I have always been passionate about self-improvement. I recognized that *The Secret* had an enormous amount of momentum. I began featuring some of the celebrated experts that appeared on the DVD as speakers at The Learning Annex and at the Wealth Expos—people like Jack Canfield, James Ray, Loral Langemeier, and Lisa Nichols. It has been a huge success, and I have decided to capitalize even further on its momentum.

Now The Learning Annex has teamed up with Jack Canfield to produce a PBS special all about *The Secret,* which will teach people how to get what they want by merely thinking in a certain way. Jack Canfield, an amazing author, enlightened teacher, and savvy businessman, is one of the driving forces behind the *Chicken Soup for the Soul* franchise, which has sold 100 million books. He has personally taught millions of people his unique formulas for success. On The Learning Annex PBS special, Jack teaches how to make more money, get in the best shape of your life, meet your soul mate, and more by shifting your mind-set and creating your own reality.

This is all part of my plan to take The Learning Annex to the billion-dollar level. I have met with broadcast executives and producers, such as Mark Burnett and Peter Guber to build programming for a Learning Annex channel. When people think of self-help, they are going to think of The Learning Annex. The self-help industry is a $19 billion dollar industry. When you think of doing anything to improve your life, I want you to think, "The Learning Annex." We are already the premier brand, and we are just getting started.

The self-help industry is just waiting for some company to own it. I intend it to be The Learning Annex. The Learning Annex has momentum. It's growing fast and understands the market. We are passionate about it, and our timing is perfect. Baby boomers are the greatest proponents of lifelong learning. People of all ages want to continue to improve themselves. Our programming simply has to be relevant to each of the demographic groups we serve. We are taking our existing momentum to go to the next level.

Once you have momentum, you have to keep it moving. Latch onto a business trend that has great momentum. Then partner with others to set big goals and let the momentum lead you to higher and higher levels.

Every day has a new possibility. Every day you can improve yourself and grow. Every day you can take yourself to a new level. Grab something with momentum that you can be passionate about. Keep working on it and amazing things will happen.

TO SUM IT UP

To be a big success in any field you need to build momentum. Momentum is all about energy and timing. When you start anything new, you have no momentum. That is when things are hard. People are not calling you. You do not seem to be getting anywhere, but if you keep at it and keep working toward your goals one day at a time, pretty soon you get into the flow of people and events. You get contacts, you gain credibility, you build a track record of success, and then things get much easier. Why? Because you have momentum, but do not take momentum for granted. If you lose your momentum, all your success ends, and things get much more difficult. It is dangerous to do anything when you have lost your momentum. Your timing is off, and people and events are no longer in your favor. So watch out to never lose your momentum.

KEY POINTS

▶ When you start something new, you have no momentum.

▶ With every action you take and every task you complete you are building momentum.

▶ When momentum reaches a critical mass, everybody is on ready alert and has you on their radar screens.

▶ When people see momentum, they want to be part of it.

▶ To get momentum, focus on a specific goal with passion and intensity.

▶ Specialized knowledge builds momentum.

▶ Getting an experienced mentor helps momentum.

▶ To keep momentum, keep challenging yourself.

▶ Remember to keep going; if you stop, your momentum will stop.

▶ Use adverse events and monumental challenges to make you stronger.

▶ Never give up on yourself.

▶ When you reach the top, keep your momentum rolling by giving back to society.

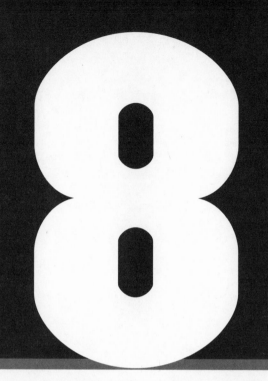

8

NEVER TAKE YOUR EYE OFF THE BALL

n 1990 I was in deep trouble. I had believed what *Business Week* wrote about me, "Everything he touches turns to gold." I said, "They are right. I'm the greatest. I'm the greatest." That was a big mistake, because when you start believing you can't fail, then you go home early; you believe that you do not have to work, and you think making money is easy.

The fact is it is not easy. After that article, I did not focus, and I did not work as hard. When the markets crashed, I was not prepared. For many years, I had made more money in bad markets than in good markets—always. This time around I was not focused. I was like a fighter who keeps winning all his fights. After a while he does not take his fights as seriously, he does not focus, and he does not train as hard because he figures he is going to win. Then out of nowhere he gets his ass kicked.

In the 90s a lot of good people went bankrupt. I never went bankrupt, but I went through hell. My company owed billions and was much too heavily leveraged. I was in debt personally for $900 million. One day I was walking down the street and I said to my then wife Marla, "That beggar over there is worth $900 million more than I am." She said, "What do you mean?" I said, "Because I'm $900 million in debt, and at least he has money in his pocket."

I used to say to myself, "Oh, my God, am I in trouble. I am going down." That was big league. I was not focused but I never blamed myself, because from the day I graduated from Wharton in 1968, I did well. For twenty-one years I was doing fantastic. I felt like I had the right to take it easy. I really felt that after twenty-one years I had the right not to focus.

Reality taught me an important lesson: I could not have it both ways. If I wanted to be the greatest, the amazing Donald Trump who makes everything he touches turn to gold, then I needed to focus. I could not have one without the other. I decided that I still wanted to be the old Trump and started focusing like never before. In 1991, the world was collapsing. It was so bad in real estate that if a person walked into a building, just looking around, we considered it to be a sign that the market was changing. They did not have to do anything; just walk in. They did not have to buy, and they did not have to rent. I came up with a statement, "Survive 'til '95." That statement was the rallying cry that helped me to stay involved and engaged even though things were really bad. After that I started to really work my ass off. Today my company is many, many times bigger, and is a much better company than it ever was before.

Someone once asked me, "What was your mind-set when you owed billions of dollars?" I answered, "My mind-set was the same as it is right now." Actually, my mind-set was very positive. I started negotiating new deals even though I was in no position to do them, because it made me feel good. Most of my real estate friends became depressed. They stopped functioning. They could not think, and they lost confidence in themselves. They were all screwed up. The best thing about being in deep financial trouble was that I learned that I could handle it, and by focusing on the positives, things that made me feel good, I could maintain a mind-set very much like it is right now. Remember that. If you ever get into deep difficulty, always focus on the things that make you feel better. Sure, handle the bad stuff you have to deal with, but do not let it demoralize you or distract you from pursuing your goals. Realize that it is only a moment in time, and it will pass. Keep your sights set on a better time in the future, which will certainly come to pass if you stay focused. Things cannot and will not continue downward forever; they will always turn around. I have seen this many times, and that is why I was able to buy the Penn Central property in 1973, when things in New York were very bad. That is how I had the foresight to buy 40 Wall Street when all the real estate experts passed it up. That is how I was able to make a comeback from the brink of utter failure.

Sure I had a few sleepless nights. Not as bad as other people, because I still managed to go to sleep, and I still managed to keep my faculties. I was able to do what I had to do. I was in a horrific period. I had been the hottest guy in the 80s. Then almost overnight, I went from being a super genius to a moron. It was a pretty hard blow, but I realized that I was not the moron that the media was making me out to be. I was the same person. I still had what it takes to be great. I never forgot that.

In truth, I simply got caught like many others when the market crashed. In all fairness, the government changed the tax laws in real estate and made those changes apply to buildings that were purchased years earlier when the tax code was different. It was unfair. That is what killed many developers. I do not blame anybody. I should have seen it coming. The market crash was just another down market, and my whole life I had made money in down markets. I blame myself, because I was not as focused as I had been in the past. I learned from this mistake. I kept a firm belief in myself that no bankers or lawyers or media reporters could dislodge. I got super focused. I went back to work and never worked harder, ever. I am still working, and I love it.

Who you marry has a big impact on your ability to focus. I will give you an example: Andre Agassi, the great tennis player, was known for his powerful forehand and aggressive style. Andre's father, Mike, a former boxer, started training Andre as soon as he was able to hold a racket. He gave little Andre paddles and balloons when he was still in a high chair. When he started playing tennis, Agassi would hit 5,000 balls every day. When Andre was five years old, he was already practicing with pros such as Jimmy Connors and Roscoe Tanner. He turned professional in 1986 and won his first top level singles title in 1987. Agassi was ranked number one in the world in April 1995 and held that ranking for thirty consecutive weeks.

In 1997 he married Brooke Shields, who I think is a fantastic person. His tennis suffered because of it. Distracted by all the media frenzy surrounding his celebrity marriage to Brooke, he lost his focus on tennis. He played only twenty-four matches, he won no titles, and his world ranking sank to an abysmal number 141. It seemed as if he was washed up and his career was over. I remember watching one of his matches at the time. His new wife, Brooke Shields, was watching, and he was losing. All of a sudden she left before the match was over. I said, "What the hell is going on?" I figured she was coming back, but she never did.

I later found out that Andre and Brooke really did not

spend much time together. Brooke spent her time in Los Angeles, while Andre lived in Las Vegas. Rumors circulated that Brooke wanted to start a family and put pressure on Andre to cool it in the tennis circuit, but Agassi would not give in to her. He rededicated himself to tennis. He began a rigorous conditioning program. He won five titles and leapt from number 141 to number 6 within a year. He divorced Brooke Shields and started dating Steffi Graf in 1999, who supported his tennis career. Shortly thereafter he took home the French Open title— a win that made him the fifth male player in tennis history to capture all four of the Grand Slam titles. He later married Steffi Graf and again became number one—she was the right woman behind the man.

Another example is my former employee, Carolyn Kepcher. When she lost her focus, I had to fire her, but it was not like one of my dramatic boardroom scenes. The fact is I like Carolyn. She worked for me for eleven years and was doing a good job managing my Trump National Golf Club in Briarcliff Manor, New York. After I started using her on *The Apprentice,* her love of fame and celebrity began affecting her work. She was not doing her job like she used to or was capable of doing. After the show became successful she became impossible for people to deal with. It went to her head. I do not think there is anything wrong with this, because I think it is human nature.

This is not the first time such a thing has happened, nor will it be the last. She was supposed to be managing the golf course. She was supposed to be selling memberships and she was not doing it. She became a prima donna. She was off giving speeches and doing product endorsement deals—that's good for her but not good for me.

I would try to get her on the phone, and she would be off giving a speech or was not at her desk. If I got her on the phone, I would ask, "How much are the belts? How much are the shirts? How much are the ties?" Her tone of voice said, "I can't believe you just asked me a question that's so boring." Before all the fame went to her head, I would ask, "How much are those shirts?" And she would tell me right away to the penny. Suddenly, the details of running a business—specifically, my business—were no longer of interest to her.

It was very clear that I had to do something. I had to get somebody to run my club. It was just one of those things that had to be done. I gave serious thought to firing her live on the air during her last season on *The Apprentice*. However, I thought it would be too tough. It was my duty to find somebody responsible, and when she lost her focus, I had to find somebody else who would devote their full time and thought process to the club.

Carolyn lost her job because she lost her focus! My rule

is to never believe what anyone says about you, good or bad, especially the media. Do not believe the bad stuff and certainly learn not to believe the good stuff. Draw your own conclusions about yourself. Listen to your own counsel. Nobody knows you better than you do. Now my club, Trump National, has new management and it is doing great—life goes on!

In 2006 Ohio State was the number one ranked college football team in the country and the darling of the media. They were "unstoppable"; "nobody could beat them;" they were "the best team ever." When it was announced that Ohio State was to play Florida in the BCS Bowl everyone said that Florida "would lose badly"; "didn't have a chance"; and "didn't even deserve to be on the same field as Ohio State."

Actually the teams were pretty well matched, but there was one big difference: Ohio State believed the media and Florida did not. Ohio State believed that it was without a doubt the better team. They believed that they had the game in the bag, and that it was going to be a blowout victory for them. In their minds they had taken all the credit for winning the game before the ball was snapped. They already thought they were the national champions. They lost the intense focus you need to win in big-time college football.

Florida, on the other hand, refused to believe the hype

about how they were a second-rate team and not worthy to be playing Ohio State. They respected Ohio State and knew they were going to be in the battle of their lives, and they prepared for it. They lived for it and trained intensely with one goal in mind: beating Ohio State and winning the national championship and it worked. Florida jumped out to a quick lead and got all the momentum. Ohio State never caught up. Florida surprised everyone by beating Ohio State in a stunning blowout victory.

If you want to become successful and stay successful, you must learn how to focus. Comedian Tim Allen is very successful now. Several decades ago he was not as successful. Allen had a substance-abuse problem. He even spent time in jail. Today he owns a production company, picks his scripts, and is a star. So his system is more than a theory. For him, at least, it has produced results.

He said that he uses three lists to maintain his focus: The first list contains the greatest goals he wants to achieve in his life; the second list has the things he needs to do this year in order to reach his life goals; and the final list keeps him focused on the things he needs to do today in order to reach his life goals. It is very simple, the key to making this system work is discipline. The ultimate winner is the man or woman who has the discipline to do this every day of their lives, without fail.

Champion chess player Bobby Fischer was passionate about staying focused on chess strategy. When asked about his technique, he said, "I don't believe in psychology. I believe in good moves." He also boasted that he gave 98 percent of his mental energy to chess, while others gave only 2 percent. That explains his success. He enjoyed the challenge of focusing his mental energy.

Every successful person has had to deal with problems. I know people who see a problem as a game to be won, and they focus on solving it. I know other people who see every problem as a burden, and they are defeated before they start. Some people carry around a lot of mental baggage, which destroys their focus. Get rid of it. It just gets in the way and slows you down.

When I was doing the first season of *The Apprentice,* I was new to TV, and I had very little knowledge of how TV shows work, how networks operate, and how ratings are determined. I also did not have the same TV-related baggage that many other TV personalities have. I did not worry that I was an unknown on TV, that I was doing a business show, and that no business show had ever been successful. I did not worry about ratings and sponsors. I just didn't consider the fact that 95 percent of all new shows fail. My lack of experience was actually a good thing, because I was free of mental baggage and worry. I just put all my concentration into what I was doing and, as problems surfaced, I dealt with them.

Too many people think too much about their current situation, instead of thinking about what could be. They are so caught up in the problem that they lose the ability to envision a solution. If you have a problem with a difficult employee, for example, and you focus on how bad the person is and how they are destroying morale in the whole office, you will lose your focus. Then you end up going over and over in your mind all their faults, and you torture yourself with how bad it is right now. You will never find a solution that way. You have lost the focus on your goals by letting your mind focus only on your difficulties.

Don't get caught up in all the crap. Acknowledge the problem, and then shift your attention immediately to possible solutions. Start by first thinking about what is good about the existing situation. Then dream up scenarios in which things are better. Then come up with as many ideas as you can of ways to attain the results you want. Write down these ideas without judging them. Do not let your mind come up with reasons why your ideas can't work. Then take the best ideas and act on them. Your constructive actions will eventually lead you to a solution. This is the Trump way of using focus to solve problems.

Do not think about the problem in terms of "How did it

happen?" or "Why did it happen?" or "It's so difficult," or "It is impossible to solve," or "What will happen if I don't solve it?" Instead, accept that you have a problem and a great challenge has been laid at your feet. Accept the challenge. Realize that you have what it takes to overcome the challenge. Then look for solutions. Study possible solutions. Gather knowledge. Ask experts for advice and insights. Formulate a plan. Start testing possible solutions. If one idea fails, go to the next one and the next until you succeed.

It is true that a few people are born to be successful. They possess some special talent that makes it easy to succeed—the gifted musician, the natural athlete, or the talented business person. The vast majority of successful people were not handed their success on a silver platter. They worked hard for it. They set goals and stayed focused on their goals until they reached them.

Focus and discipline are habits, skills that everyone can learn. I was the most undisciplined kid you could ever imagine. My parents could not handle me so they sent me off to a military school at a young age, where I learned discipline. Without this training, I never would have become who I am today.

Worry, fear, and indecision destroy focus. To take charge of your life you must conquer fear. My advice is simply to zap every negative thought as soon as it shows its ugly face. Stop the indecisive internal dialogue before it starts. That is your biggest enemy. You can have enemies at your door, deal with financial crises, fight legal battles, and face the biggest difficulties in life, and none of these things will have any effect on you if you control your mental dialogue.

When people try to distract me or frighten me by saying, "What if the market goes bad?" or "What if the banks call your loans?" or "What if everything goes bad?" I just say, "I don't want to think about it." The worst hell you will ever face is the hell you create with your own mind. It is much worse than the hell other people create for you. So instead of dwelling on all the negatives, think about what you want. Think about all the good things you are going to do in life. Keep focused on your goal and never give up. Besides, bad times bring great opportunities.

Focus is a tricky thing. Focus does not mean that you narrow your mind and become inflexible. That is taking focus way too far. Just recently I attended the Emmy Awards in Los Angeles because *The Apprentice* was nominated for Best Reality Show. I was also asked to sing the *Green Acres* theme song with Megan Mullally, dressed in overalls and a straw hat and holding a pitchfork.

This was not really my thing. I am no Tony Bennett, Frank Sinatra, or Elton John. At that time I was focused on making

The Apprentice a success, as the star and co-producer. I could have easily said, "No," because I am not really a singer. I did it though and as a result I won the talent category for the night beating out five other big movie star types including the wonderful William Shatner. I would not have had this wonderful experience if I had not been flexible.

I pride myself on being obstinate, stubborn, and tough. I think those are important qualities found in successful people. Sometimes, however, you need to ease up and relax a bit, while staying focused on your overall goals. Do not confuse being focused with being stiff and inflexible. You need to be flexible. You need to be able to adjust to continually changing circumstances if you want to win the tough battles in business and in life. Being overly rigid in your thinking and your habits will not get you to the top. Accepting a fixed pattern places limits on you and your future.

There are more ways to achieve the brass ring than you might think. It is not always a straight shot to success. The world is in an amazing state of constant flux and change. Your road to the top will have a great number of detours, changes in direction, twists and turns. Expect an exciting, adventurous ride on your way to the top. It is interesting, it is fun, and it is definitely not predictable! Trying to narrow it down to something you can predict and understand will limit your growth. Like a surfer, you have to learn how to ride the waves.

Do your daily routine, but keep yourself available for pleasant surprises and always be ready to turn on a dime when good luck comes your way. When Mark Burnett came to me with the idea for *The Apprentice,* I could have brushed him off without even listening to him, because I was already very busy. When he brought up the subject I really was not interested because I had been approached for shows before, and I always turned them down. After I listened to him, I realized his idea was different, and I really liked it. I am certainly glad I was flexible enough to listen to his idea.

Another thing to keep in mind—while remaining focused on the task at hand—is that there are events we cannot control. Natural catastrophes, terrorist attacks, and wars happen. Do not be so rigid that you can be broken; it is wiser to be pliable. Keep your equilibrium by being aware of the positives along with the negatives, and be adaptable enough to adjust to what comes along. One negative happened with *The Apprentice,* it was more than once nominated for an Emmy, and its first nomination, for the first season, was easily anticipated to win. Everybody was stating that nobody else had a chance. I was asked to go to California by NBC, Mark Burnett, and everybody else to pick up the Emmy. I really thought this was cool because who would of thought that Donald Trump, a real estate developer who just happened to do a television show, would now be getting the Emmy?

In any event, the show totally deserved the Emmy, it was well made, the talk of the country. It was one of the hottest shows on television, the most successful reality show in the history of NBC, and not that this matters, the total darling of the advertisers. At the Emmy Awards, they went down the list of the four or five competitors *The Apprentice* had, and announced the winner, a show which has never been very good, but always seems to get Emmys, *Amazing Race*. The audience was stunned, as was I. In fact, it was a little embarrassing because just prior to the announcement I started to stand up in order to get ready for the walk to the stage. I knew exactly what I was going to say, but the thing that I most remember about that evening was a great man named Sir Howard Stringer, who is the head of Sony and sitting four rows behind me, got up from his seat, walked over to where I was sitting on the aisle and whispered into my ear, "Donald, you got screwed," and then immediately sat back down.

I was disappointed, but then realized that I am not part of the Emmy establishment and it's justifiably hard for them to give an Emmy to someone like me rather than the *Amazing Race* establishment that probably worked the Emmy system very hard. I don't know why, but it was an embarrassing moment for me. Nevertheless I acted as though nothing happened and within two days it was all forgotten. *The Apprentice* got other Emmy nominations, but likewise, never won—not that it shouldn't have, but that's the way the system works.

When I was building the now-famous Trump Tower back in the early 80s, I wanted to name it Tiffany Tower because it is adjacent to Tiffany's on Fifth Avenue. A friend asked me why I was going to name my building after a famous jewelry store when in fact it was my building. It was a good point, so I changed the name. Now Trump Tower is one of the most important tourist destinations in New York. It pays to listen and to be willing to change your mind.

Life is unpredictable, the world is unpredictable, and there is no reason our goals should keep us from changing and growing along with it. Focus on the evolving world, and you will keep in touch with what is happening now. Do not limit yourself! Realize that goals are not fixed patterns, act accordingly, and your versatility will serve you well.

ZANKER'S TAKE

You have to keep your focus and never give up. In 1985 *USA Today* put out thousands of street boxes all over the five boroughs of New York City and New Jersey where people could pick up copies of the newspaper each day. Although there was no ordinance against it, Mayor Koch said, "Those boxes must go." Gannett, the owner of *USA Today,* sued the city to have the boxes stay. One day I read in the paper that Gannett won the suit. The judge ruled that Gannett could keep all the boxes in place for a $1 fee.

I wanted to put out boxes so we could distribute copies of The Learning Annex catalog. When I read this article, I saw my opportunity. I quickly put down thousands of boxes all over New York City, just like *USA Today* and I sent a certified check for $1. Then I got a call from the city saying, "You can't do this." I said, "Why?" I refused to remove the boxes. Then I got a notice that the city of New York was suing me to force me to remove the boxes. But I would not budge.

We took it all the way to New York's highest court, the Court of Appeals. And when we got there, I won. Just like Gannett, I was allowed to keep all my boxes in place. The boxes are still there, and we have boxes in major cities like Chicago, Los Angeles, San Diego, Minneapolis, San Francisco, and Toronto. I stayed focused and refused to quit and it paid off big time!

Because our Wealth Expos are so successful, we started getting offers. Every offer you can imagine. And because we had Donald as our keynote, everyone wanted to do something with us. At first we were all excited, running from one idea to the next. It was all so intriguing after years of working so hard and not getting recognition. But I started noticing that the team was getting distracted. We were all running after different opportunities fast and furious, and we were not watching our business. So I got the team together after we had done a huge expo in San Francisco and asked, "Where do we want to be in thirty months?" And we decided we needed to get our own Learning Annex channel. So I said we needed to stay focused spending 80 percent of our time on our core business, while we pursue this new business. All other opportunities just had to wait. It was a painful decision, but I knew we had to stay focused.

Everyone thinks that to do $100 million in sales, you need a big organization. Since we all share in the profits, we don't like to be too big. And, in fact, we are almost the same size as when we were doing $10 million in sales. Obviously, we are a very profitable small organization.

When we started The Learning Annex Wealth Expo business I met with the president of a large publicly held company that trades on the New York stock exchange that did expos around the world. This president was so full of himself that he laughed out loud when I told him what we intended to do. He said, "Six of you are going to bring in ten thousand people and you have no experience. Impossible." He called us the "desperados." I came back to the office and called the "desperados" together in our tiny conference room and told them what this fat slob president had just called us. It was great. It was our rallying cry and unified us against this bigger company.

So when he saw that we brought in not 10,000 students, but over 30,000 students he tried to rip us off. He tried to do his own type of money show and he got less than 2,000 people. He had no passion and his organization was as bloated as he was. I saw recently he was fired and the new president wrote me a nice letter asking how we could work together.

There is a song I always hum to myself when things are going good. "Just when you think you're hot, you're not." So I never allow myself to get complacent. We are always "almost hot."

TO SUM UP

If you want to become successful and stay successful, you must learn how to focus. Becoming successful is very hard. You are going to run into many problems and obstacles. Instead of dwelling on all the negatives, think about what you want. Think about all the good things you are going to do in life. Keep focused on your goal and never give up. You can never rest no matter how good things are going. Your current "good times" are only a result of the hard work and dedication you have.

If you want to continue being successful, you've got to keep doing the things that got you there in the first place. If you let yourself get distracted by all the trappings of success you're sowing the seeds of your own decline. So never stop focusing on your goals, no matter how successful you are.

It is true that a few people are born to be successful. They possess some special talent that makes it easy to succeed—the gifted musician, the natural athlete, or the talented business person. However, the vast majority of successful people weren't handed their success on a silver platter. They worked hard for it. They set goals, and stayed focused on their goals until they reached them.

It's a fact that you may be able to coast your way to success because of some special talent or ability that you were born with. However, most of the time you will need to work hard and stay focused to get to the top—and then work even harder to stay there. Start with the natural talent you were born with. Then use your determination through the good and tough times to reach your goals and achieve amazing things in your life.

KEY POINTS

▶ Remember that success is never easy.

▶ Always take your work seriously.

▶ Keep focusing on doing what you love, even if times are tough.

▶ Acknowledge your problems, but focus on what feels good.

▶ Time is on your side; things do not continue downward forever.

▶ Who you marry can impact your ability to focus.

▶ He or she who focuses the longest wins.

▶ Focus and discipline are habits that everyone can learn.

▶ Worry destroys focus.

▶ Be flexibly focused. Focus does not mean being narrow-minded or rigid.

▶ Be pliable enough to adjust to changing circumstances.

9

I LOVE YOU, SIGN THIS

Always have a prenuptial agreement. I have seen people and businesses destroyed because there wasn't a prenup. I will be honest with you, if I did not have prenuptial agreements with Ivana and Marla, I would not have anything now. They attacked me rather viciously. Fortunately, I had prenuptial agreements. I did my wheeling and dealing and today my company is much bigger, much stronger, and much richer than ever before. If I had not had prenuptial agreements, it would not be that way. I probably would have lost everything.

Actually, I get along very well with my ex-wives. I think you have an obligation to your children to get along. Ivana and Marla are both terrific women. I don't blame them at all. The failure of these marriages was my fault. What happened was my fault. It is hard to be a success; to own your own business or to hold a stressful, high-paying job. Frankly, it is very hard on your family. Ivana and Marla were both great, but they could not compete with my business. Business is so all-encompassing to me. I love it! I leave home early in the morning. I come home late at night. I did not see my ex-wives as often as they deserved.

Now, when you get married, you think you are in love. Nobody thinks, "I'm getting married, but I know I'm going to get divorced." I know you are in love, but do not let it cloud your judgment. The reality is that 58 percent of marriages end up in divorce. You want to go out and create a great business, buy some real estate, or build your assets. You can't do that knowing that 58 percent of the time people get divorced. If you get married without a prenup, there is a 58 percent chance you will get a divorce and lose everything, even if you were madly in love when you get married in the first place. As one divorce lawyer put it, "Made in heaven, settled in court." It is sad and ugly, but true!

I have seen bad deals and bad partnerships. I have seen lots of business deals in litigation—and litigation is not nice. There is nothing worse than a man and a woman that are fighting, especially when they are fighting over their assets, their children, their business, their home, their cars, and everything else. It's terrible. You are in love with somebody, and then realize you are in a war. The battle is so intense; far more intense than it gets in a business transaction. There is nothing more vicious than a man or a woman going through a divorce. It is pure hell, like nothing I have ever seen. You need a prenuptial agreement. You need certainty.

As a businessman, I've seen a lot of terrible litigation. Deals go bad, partnerships break up, and all hell breaks loose. People fight brutally over deals and property. It's nothing compared to the fight between a man and a woman, who used to be in love and sometimes still are. The hatred is more intense than any business litigation I've ever seen.

Love blinds most couples to the truth, and they refuse to face the fact that something bad could happen between them. It takes an exceptional couple to face up to this harsh reality and sign a prenuptial agreement. If you're planning to get married, be the exception. It's just stupid not to protect yourself from the living hell you will very likely have to go through if you don't have one. You always need a prenuptial agreement.

Sometimes things get way out of control. I know a couple of cases where one spouse did absolutely nothing, and the other spouse worked eighteen hours a day for years. In the end, the spouse that did nothing sues for all the money, hundreds of millions of dollars. I say, "Give me a break."

This friend of mine is the toughest guy I know, but he is a schmuck when it comes to women. When this guy walks down the street, other men cross to the other side of the street. He is just a rough guy. A woman who is five foot four can wrap him around her finger like a rubber band. He has been married four times, and he never had a prenup. Every time he got divorced, he settled for $50 million. He has divorced four different women, and he paid $50 million to each one of them. It was always the same amount.

Last year he called me and he told me, "Donald, I want to tell you something. I met the most unbelievable woman and we are getting married." I said, "Are you going to get a prenuptial agreement?" He said, "I don't think I'll need one, Donald. This woman is fantastic. She's the love of my life." I said, "That's what you told me four times already." He said, "No, this is different." I said, "Where did you meet her?" He said, "In Las Vegas. She's a showgirl." He is a brutal killer, a business genius, an absolute animal who rips people apart, but when it comes to women, he is an absolute idiot. I said, "You have zero chance of this marriage lasting."

I was even more sure of it after I met the woman and she came after me. She was chasing after me and he thinks she is this great woman; the love of his life who will be married to him till death do they part. What a joke! She found me more attractive than him, and he is telling me what a great marriage he will have. He is in for trouble because he does not have a prenup. You need to have a prenuptial agreement. I call it a certainty agreement. It gives you certainty. If you are building a business, you need a certainty agreement to define who gets what if you split.

Look at Paul McCartney, the poor bastard. This ex-Beatle is one of the greatest musical stars of our time. He has sold millions and millions of recordings and became a millionaire many times over. Supposedly, he is worth $1.5 billion. Then his wife Linda died of breast cancer, and he married Heather Mills. Who ever heard of Heather Mills? Some people said she was a nude model in the 80s and worked for an escort service. Who knows the truth? The point is she was a nobody. Now that she has been on *Dancing with the Stars,* she is better known. If she had not married Paul McCartney she would still be a nobody. I remember watching Larry King before Paul and Heather were married. Larry King said, "Sir Paul, are you going to have a prenuptial agreement?" He said, "I'd never have one, Larry. I don't want one, because we're deeply in love, and I don't want one." I thought, "What a mistake. This guy's a schmuck." I heard that Heather even offered to sign a prenuptial agreement and he turned it down.

Sure as hell she made his life miserable for three years, then sued him for $400 million. I think she got 60 million dollars, plus his home in St. John's Wood. That is not bad for three years. I said to myself, "Isn't that really ridiculous?"

Remember last year when Paul and Heather McCartney announced they were getting divorced and they said they would split "amicably" for the sake of their three-year-old daughter, Beatrice? I said no way and was right. The gloves eventually came off and things got really nasty. After that, Paul changed the locks on his London mansion and froze their joint bank account. He even issued a legal letter claiming that his soon-to-be-ex removed three bottles of cleaning fluid from his home. I am not sure why that matters, but the accusation went public.

In court documents, Paul claims that Heather was "argumentative" and "rude to the staff" during their marriage. Because they had no prenuptial agreement, she was pushing to get 400 million dollars in the divorce.

There are reports that Heather was running around with a camcorder, shooting everything that happened to her. Allegedly, she is going to use the tapes against Paul to get more money. Or she is going to make a documentary about how she has been the poor, wronged victim in this whole ordeal in order to sway public support. The bottom line is she went after a huge chunk of Paul's money. She even destroyed the myth or fact of Paul's great marriage to Linda by disparaging it.

I know I sound like a broken record but when people have money—whether they are famous or not—they have to protect that money, no matter how much in love they think they are. Get a prenuptial agreement. I do not care how much you love your fiancé; it is just idiotic to get married without one. Don't believe me? Ask Paul McCartney what he thinks. I bet he wishes he had one.

Last year I spoke to a group of 20,000 people in Atlanta for The Learning Annex. A gorgeous woman got up to ask me if she could audition for *The Apprentice*. Let's call her Jennifer. The second I laid eyes on her I knew she was hot, hot, hot! I said, "Come on up here to the podium, Jennifer. You're hired."

She came up to the stage, and she brought her sister who was equally gorgeous. I asked, "Are you both from Atlanta? Are you both married?" Jennifer was married and her sister was single. I asked Jennifer, "Is your husband here?" She said, "no." I said, "Okay, there are only about 20,000 people here, and he's never going to find out. Have you ever cheated on your husband?" Jennifer said, "Truthfully, yes. I have to say that it was the worst thing I've ever done in my life, and I hope he'll forgive me."

The crowd went wild and the sister gasped in surprise and said she did not even know about her sister's affair. I said, "In front of all of these people, you admit you cheated like a dog." Jennifer said, "I do not lie." I said, "Do you have any friends here other than your sister? Because if you do, please tell them not to report you; that's the end of your marriage. Does your husband know about it?" She replied, "No." I said, "Do you have a prenuptial agreement?" She said, "No. I make more money than my husband." I said, "You are going to need one." The next question asked by an attendee was, "Where are interest rates going?" "How boring," I said.

I have been talking about the importance of prenuptial agreements for many years, and maybe people are starting to listen. For example, I read that the Equality in Marriage Institute now get about 5,000 inquiries a month about prenups, up from only 1,500 just a few years ago.

One out of ten first-time married couples get prenups. Nine out of ten couples are living in a fool's paradise, expecting a life of eternal wedded bliss. After that first divorce, many of them wise up. One out of five couples get prenups before their second, third, or fourth marriages. That is amazing: after three divorces a full 80 percent still refuse to have a prenup.

It seems that a whole lot of people never want to get a prenuptial agreement. Why? Forty-three percent of them say they do not need a prenup because, get this, "They don't plan to ever get divorced." That's stupid. Who ever plans to get a divorce when they are first getting married? Nobody.

Five percent of people who do not get a prenup, are afraid of asking their spouse for a prenup. They think their fiancé will refuse to sign and call off the wedding. I know, it is a horrible thing to have happen, but there are worse things, like losing all your money.

When I heard that Nick Lachey and Jessica Simpson were splitting up I was not surprised. People change quickly, especially when they are in their twenties. They are still discovering who they are. When Nick and Jessica first met, his career was bigger than hers. After their reality TV show her career really took off and his did too, but to a lesser extent.

Nick and Jessica did not sign a prenuptial agreement. Jessica's father has done a great job managing Jessica's career. I can't understand why he did not insist that the couple get a prenup.

Jessica and Nick were hoping for a nice, amicable divorce. Surprise, surprise, it did not happen that way. Nick asked for alimony and a lot of it. He wanted 50 percent of Jessica's money. She made an estimated $35 million in 2005 alone. It wasn't pleasant. When it was all said and done in December 2006, I'll bet Nick got a big chunk of cash.

You should have a prenup. I know it sounds terrible, and there is nothing romantic about it. It is a hard subject to talk about with someone you love. Where a lot of money and assets are concerned, it is vital. You never know about love, but you do know that when the love is gone there will be a knock-down, drag-out fight over the assets. It always happens, unless you have a prenup.

In your business, you always determine ahead of time what will happen if the business relationship comes to an end. It is the responsible thing to do. Why not do the same thing with your personal relationship? Sure, it is not pleasant, but it makes a lot of sense to define how things will be divided if the two of you call it quits. A prenup can spare you most of the messiest, most unpleasant aspects of a divorce.

These days, a prenup is just as important to women as it is to men. I have seen many cases recently, where a woman makes a lot of money and the man does not, and the woman ends up having to pay big money to the husband.

The fact is, whether you are a man or a woman, you need the certainty. It is really important. You always have to expect problems. You can solve the problem in advance before it happens with the certainty of a prenuptial agreement. Settle while you are friends, not enemies.

In all honesty, it is not pretty. A prenuptial agreement is a horrible instrument. I met Melania, and we fell in love and decided to get married. I said, "Melania, you are so beautiful, I love you so much, and we're going to have the greatest marriage ever. It's going to be unbelievable. Listen, just in case it doesn't work, sign on the dotted line." It is not exactly the most romantic thing to do, but you really, really need it.

ZANKER'S TAKE

There are many people I do business with on a handshake. I trust them and they trust me. We still write down what we agreed to, even if it is just an email. We write down the basics of the agreement so that neither of us will feel taken advantage of, confused about the relationship, or resentful that the other person forgot an important term. I call that an "email handshake." The reason is that it is so easy to forget what we agreed to. It is not that we are ever going to fight over something, and it is not necessary in these situations to have a big formal contract that involves lawyers and has all the "what ifs" and says which state law is going to apply if one of us sues the other.

I learned the importance of this the hard way. I once saw an ad in *The Wall Street Journal* that a bunch of ski condos were being auctioned off. I investigated and thought it was a good deal. That week I was having dinner with a friend—let's call him Howard—and mentioned I was flying to the auction the next day. He said, "If it is a good deal, buy one for me, too." He gave me a down payment check on the spot. I immediately said, "Okay, but listen, since I am doing all the work on this one, just promise me that if you ever sell, you will give me the right of first refusal." He agreed. I finished up the due diligence for both of us, and the next day bid successfully on two condos.

A couple of years later, I was going on a ski vacation to my condo, and I called Howard because I needed to rent his condo to some friends who were joining us. "The ski condo?" he said. "I sold it a couple of months ago. I got a great price." I did not say anything; I just congratulated Howard on making a good deal. I was seething inside. He probably forgot, and if he did, it is probably because we did not bother to write down our little deal. I should have at least done an "email handshake."

I introduced a very, very good friend of mine to an acquaintance in the late 80s. They didn't like each other at first but I kept on insisting they would get along and create great business together. In fact, I proposed that all three of us would be very powerful doing a deal together. They didn't like each other no matter how hard I tried. Then the two of them met at a fund-raiser and got to be friends. A few months later I see they are doing business together, and they completely cut me out. They didn't even tell me. I just happened to hear about it. I was furious. I called my friend on it and he had the nerve to say, "But we didn't have a written contract between us." I was livid. I hung up the phone on him. I never talked to my friend again and nine months later he died of a heart attack at a young age. I always wonder if screwing me was worth it to him and if the stress of treating people that way contributed to his heart attack. Maybe it was just the bad karma I was sending him.

TO SUM IT UP

Many people go into marriage with blinders on, thinking that nothing will ever go wrong. They would not dream of buying a house without a guarantee from the owner, covering them if something goes wrong. When it comes to marriage, the old saying is still true, "Love is blind." The truth is that there is a 58 percent chance your marriage will fail, and you will end up divorced. Very few people plan for it because they are afraid to confront the subject when they are so in love. A prenup is a horrible document, there is nothing nice about it, but it is much better than the alternative.

KEY POINTS

▶ People's lives get destroyed because they did not have a prenup.

▶ Fifty-eight percent of marriages end in divorce.

▶ Do not let love cloud your judgment.

▶ There is nothing more terrible than a man and a woman, who use to love each other, clawing at each other's throats over money and property.

▶ Both men and women need prenups.

▶ Nobody plans on getting divorced.

▶ A prenup is a certainty agreement that defines what happens in case of a divorce.

▶ A prenup is not the most romantic thing to do, but you really need it.

10

THINK BIG AND KICK ASS IN BUSINESS AND LIFE

No matter what you do, think big. Thinking big is the driving force that has forged all the great achievements in modern life, from the towering skyscrapers to the amazing discoveries in science, technology, and medicine to the great industrial and military achievements. Thinking big is behind every successful business, church, and political organization. Thinking big is what creates loving and lasting relationships.

I believe that if you focus on the top, you will get there. Some people have the innate ability to get to the top. They are born champions. Other champions are self-made. Tiger Woods is one of them. So are Michael Jordan and Derek Jeter and Tom Brady and Big Ben Roethlisberger among others. They use discipline and determination to overcome obstacles and beat the odds. They set their sights on achieving something big. Ordinary would not be enough. They think big and work toward big goals.

In a lot of ways it is easier to do things on a large scale. It is easier to build a skyscraper in Manhattan than it is to buy a bungalow in the Bronx. For one thing, it takes just as much time to close a big deal as it does to close a small deal. You will endure as much stress and aggravation; you will have all the same headaches and problems. It is easier to finance a big deal. Bankers would much rather lend money for a big project than for a small one. They are more comfortable investing money in a big prestigious building than they are a rundown house in a bad section of town. If you succeed with the big project, you stand to gain a lot more money.

The first step to success is to make the leap from being nobody to being somebody. Most people are afraid to think big. They just can't do it. Why? Because they cannot imagine themselves doing big things; they do not have the knowledge, experience, or track record. They have none of the trappings that a successful big-thinking person has. When it comes to thinking big, you are your own worst enemy.

Do you believe that thinking big is reserved for people with money, college degrees, family connections, or even intelligence? That is not true. Anyone can think big. The most important thing is the size of your thinking. How big you think determines how big a success you become. Everything else is secondary. The simple act of thinking big immediately distinguishes you from the vast majority of people. So start now. First find a big goal for yourself, then mold yourself to become the person who can accomplish that goal.

I decided to be a big developer. So, I worked at becoming the person who could handle big development projects. I went to Wharton and learned all about finance and money. I studied real estate in my spare time. I worked for five years with my father, learning how to make deals and build quality buildings faster and cheaper than anyone else.

Then I felt I was ready to take on bigger challenges. So I moved to Manhattan and started my company. I had a big goal, and I took all the steps to become the somebody who could achieve that goal.

WALK SOFTLY AND CARRY A BIG ATTITUDE

Adopt a big attitude to go with your big thinking. Everything you do in life, do with attitude. I always think of myself as the best-looking guy and it is no secret that I love beautiful women. That is why I bought the *Miss USA* and *Miss Universe* pageants. I love being around beautiful women. My wife does not mind because she is the most beautiful woman of all—and she knows I married her because I love her and I wanted to marry her. I had a choice of staying single or getting married, and I chose to be married. I do not want to be single. I have a bad track record for being married, it is true, but I would rather live a married life than be single. That is because I met the right woman. I have learned something from my previous mistakes. I am determined to do much better in my marriage to Melania.

What surprises many people is that beautiful women love me. For the first season of *The Apprentice* NBC paid me almost nothing and nobody expected that it would make it. They would not even waste money on the ink to sign an option agreement with me. One broadcast exec said, "To be successful, large numbers of women would have to watch, and why would women want to watch Donald Trump?" I said, "I have not done so badly with women." As it turned out, the biggest audience for *The Apprentice* by far is women.

The women I have dated over the years could have any man they want; they are the top models and most beautiful women in the world. I have been able to date (screw) them all because I have something that many men do not have. I don't know what it is but women have always liked it. So guys, be cocky, confident, smart, and humorous and you will be able to get all the women you want.

Geraldo Rivera is a friend of mine, but he did something which I thought was absolutely terrible and he admits it was a mistake. He wrote a book naming many of the famous women that he slept with. I would never do that—I have too much respect for women in general, but if I did, the world would take serious notice. Beautiful, famous, successful, married—I've had them all, secretly, the world's biggest names, but unlike Geraldo I don't talk about it. If I did, this book would sell 10 million copies (maybe it will anyway). The one thing I have learned with women over the years—they want it (sex!) more than we do.

We may live in houses in the suburbs but our minds and emotions are still only a short step out of the jungle. In primitive times women clung to the strongest males for protection. They did not take any chances with a nobody, low-status male who did not have the means to house them, protect them, and feed them and their offspring. High-status males displayed their prowess through their kick-ass attitudes. They were not afraid to think for themselves and make their own decisions. They did not give a crap about what other people in the tribe thought. That kind of attitude was and still is associated with the kind of men women find attractive. It may not be politically correct to say but who cares. It is common sense and it's true—and always will be.

Oftentimes when I was sleeping with one of the top women in the world I would say to myself, thinking about me as a boy from Queens, "Can you believe what I am getting?"

The same thing goes for women. When it comes to being an attractive woman, there is no denying that looks are important. Looks alone will not get you the high-quality man you want or not for very long. Looks are only half the game. You need a big attitude to go with your good looks. A woman's attractiveness has much to do with her attitude about herself. Believe you are valuable and convey that belief in the way you stand, walk, talk, move, and use your eyes. My advice for both men and women is this: believe in yourself and show it in your attitude and you will be much more attractive to the opposite sex and if you are gay, nothing changes—it's all about attitude!

Use your big thinking attitude for work, for play, and for everything you do in life. Whatever you do, do first class with a big attitude. Some people complain that their life is boring. My life is never boring. If you want more excitement in life, it is up to you to get it. Let's say you are planning a social event. You have a choice: you can plan a modest event or you can do something big. If you plan something modest and uneventful, that is what you will get. Plan a social event and do it up big. Boost the excitement level up to top notch! Go all out to make it bigger than life and over the top.

You are what you think you are. Most people think too little of themselves and devalue their own abilities. They give other people credit for being a lot smarter than they really are, and downplay their own intelligence. Reverse this: give yourself credit for being smarter than most other people, because it is true. Let that be reflected in your attitude about yourself.

Everybody talks about George Clooney and how good-looking he is, but when I met him for drinks recently with the great Florida developer George Perez, I was surprised at how little and short he was. He was very nice but much different in stature than I thought, much different from his image. He looks much bigger on screen. Another one who is very different from her image is Angelina Jolie. For some reason I find her to be not good-looking in any way and yet the press fawns over her. I am pretty good when it comes to looks and certainly she is not a bad-looking woman, but she is no beauty. Perception is very important—the perception is that she is a great beauty; the fact is, she is not. Oftentimes, perception is more important than fact. In her case, it is.

People take their cues from you as to how they should think about you. Your attitude about yourself is visible to everyone. Develop an attitude that you are worth a lot, and others will value you. Walk briskly and purposefully, eyes looking straight ahead, like someone who knows where he or she is going. Define yourself in a big way. We all have self-definitions; give yourself a big definition.

Instead of a marketing manager, define yourself as a marketing manager on the way to becoming marketing vice president. Instead of a builder of single-family homes, define yourself as a builder of single-family homes on the way to becoming a multi-unit developer. Instead of a law assistant, define yourself as a law assistant on the way to becoming a law partner. Instead of an accountant, define yourself as an accountant on the way to becoming a financial vice president.

Display a big-thinking attitude that shows you are an active, enthusiastic, decisive, efficient, committed, important person who believes in him or herself. You are someone who wins promotions, clients, friends; someone who is moving up in life, and who is sought after for your creative ideas. Your attitude is much more important than your IQ.

Big thinkers draw positive conclusions about things. Form the habit of drawing positive conclusions. Start every day thinking, "Today is a great day. I live in the greatest nation on earth. I have a great profession. It is great to be alive. There are plenty of opportunities for me to be successful today." Then your mind will come up with reasons why it is true. Small-thinking people who draw negative conclusions will find that their minds will bring them lots of negative thoughts. It is your choice. Choose the positive.

GO FIRST CLASS ALL THE WAY

Cement your big-thinker persona by going first class all the way. Let the shoes, suits, shirts, ties, coats, and accessories such as watches and jewelry tell the world that you understand and value quality. If you do not have a big budget right now, buy fewer items, but better quality. Let everything you do and own convey an image of importance. Own a first-class car, carry first-class luggage, go to first-class restaurants, and shop in first-class stores.

I learned this lesson when I bought a football team in New Jersey. The New Jersey Generals were part of a little league called the United States Football League. I signed Doug Flutie and Herschel Walker for the 1985 season. In 1986 we filed a $1.5 billion antitrust lawsuit against the NFL claiming that the NFL conspired to monopolize football.

We won, but we only got $1 trebled, plus interest for a total of $3.76. Later we collected $6 million in legal fees. I thought it might be an inexpensive way into the NFL. I did not spend a great deal of money, and I gave it a shot. In the end I would have been better off paying up, going first class, and buying an NFL team. It is like buying Fifth Avenue real estate. It is the way to go. I learned something from that whole USFL experience— go first class!

When I married Melania in January 2005, people said,

"Donald, you have had big weddings before, why don't you have a little private ceremony with some close friends and family?" Sure, I was busy, and had a lot of things on my plate, but life is not all about business. You also have to take the time to live. I live big. I said, "No way. This is an opportunity to celebrate and have fun. It's Melania's big day, and mine, too, and I want to make it special and exciting for her and for all our friends and family."

DITCH YOUR DOUBTS

Big thinkers conquer their doubts. Doubt leads directly to failure. If you do not know how things are going to turn out, you are not alone. None of us really know. You could be hit by a bus crossing the street. Nobody knows. When in doubt, believe in yourself and assume that you will succeed. Nobody can do this for you. Do not grab for someone else's reassurance when you are feeling inadequate. Develop your own self-belief.

Oftentimes you will see somebody that is not likely to be successful, but becomes successful only because he or she has the ability to think big. A case in point is former President Jimmy Carter. He is a very nice man, but he wasn't my kind of president. I was more into the Ronald Reagans of the world.

Nevertheless, after President Carter's term as President was up, he asked to meet me and of course I agreed. I didn't know what he wanted in that I had never supported him and was actually very vocal on how poorly he handled our captives in Iran. As an example, when it was announced Ronald Reagan won the election, the Iranians immediately turned them over to us. If Jimmy Carter had won, they'd probably still be there.

Nevertheless, we had a wonderful conversation prior to getting to his point, which was, would I consider making a $50 million contribution to the Jimmy Carter Library? Here was a man that I had not supported, had not voted for, and yet he was in my office asking for a $50 million contribution! I said to myself, and told the story many times, that Jimmy Carter, despite his image to the contrary, had an ability to think big. That's why he ran for President and others did not. As it turned out, Jimmy Carter is one of the few people who did a much better job after his Presidential term than he did during it.

Another example, on the opposite side, is Mario Cuomo. I supported Mario Cuomo for many years, and after he was out of office, when I asked him for a modest and totally positive favor, he did not do it. That showed great disloyalty to me because I was in fact so loyal to him. In any event, at the time, he was the choice to run against the first President Bush. Had he run, sadly for the country, he probably would have won. He would have been a terrible president, but he didn't have the ability to think big, and at that time Bush's poll ratings were very good. As it turned out, a brilliant guy and friend of mine from Arkansas, Bill Clinton, ran and won. He has the ability to think big, and his wife, Hillary, who is a fantastic person, also has the ability to think big. That's why Bill Clinton won the election. When others were unwilling to tread against those huge poll numbers of George Bush, Bill Clinton had no fear. When Bush's numbers dropped like a rock, he was in a position to win and he took advantage of that position. Bill Clinton is a great guy with courage, Mario Cuomo is a disloyal guy without courage.

People will take their cues from you. If you believe you can do something, other people will believe it too. Give off the attitude that you are important and worth listening to. People are busy thinking about themselves. They will take a quick look at your face to see if you think you are valuable and important to yourself, and they will accept your opinion of yourself. They will see by your face and your bearing that you are self-powered, a leader who makes things happen. If you value yourself, others will respect and value you. The lion is afraid of the little lion tamer not the big strong guy who shows fear of the lion. Do not look for approval from others. That is a sure sign of weakness. Many people will be jealous or perceive you as a threat. Many people cave in and hide their light under a barrel rather than standing up to the pressure of displaying a big thinkers attitude. Do not give in.

Your belief generates the power, the skill, and the energy to succeed at achieving your goals. Doubt saps your will to succeed and signals to everyone involved that you are going to fail. Abolish all doubts! I am not talking about putting on airs or acting arrogant. Simply believe in your own competence and worth. Make an accurate assessment of your strengths and abilities and match your attitude to your abilities.

HAVING A BIG EGO IS A GOOD THING

Somebody once asked me, "What's the difference between a blowhard or a braggart and somebody that gets it done?" I recall a time when Mohammed Ali used to get up and say, "I'm the greatest. I'm going to whoop you, I'm going to destroy you." to his opponents. Ali was fighting George Foreman in the famous "Rumble in the Jungle." George, at the time, was invincible. He couldn't be beaten. He was the hardest puncher Ali ever fought. He punched harder than Joe Frazier or Sonny Liston. He could take the hardest punches and would never go down. Also, he was much younger than Mohammed.

George Foreman was such a great fighter that he knocked

out Joe Frazier and knocked him down six times. Mohammed Ali was past his prime. What he went out and did that night was amazing. Ali was smart. He had watched videos of Foreman's previous fights and he didn't tell anybody, not even his trainer. He watched a video of Foreman fighting three people in one night. Foreman knocked the first guy out immediately. These were all journeyman fighters. The fight with the second guy was closer, but he knocked him out after four rounds. In the fight with the third guy, Foreman almost did not win. He had a hard time. Mohammed saw this and he knew Foreman's weakness—he gets tired.

For five rounds of the fight, Ali didn't throw a punch. Ali did the "rope-a-dope," and just leaned on the ropes and let Foreman throw punches to his body. Foreman had trouble hitting his face. Angelo Dundee, his trainer said, "Champ, champ, we can't let you take this anymore." Ali said, "What are you crazy? I'm doing great." They did not know what he was talking about. By the fifth round Foreman was finished. Then all of a sudden in the sixth round, Ali started pummeling Foreman who had nothing left. Foreman was completely helpless and Ali knocked him out in the eighth round. This was the greatest fight ever! Mohammed Ali talks big but he also delivers the goods. My advice is yes, have a big ego, but do not be egotistical. A big ego is a positive thing.

Some other great examples of people who get it done are George Steinbrenner, Bob Kraft, and Bob Tisch. George has taken the New York Yankees to tremendous success, as have Bob Kraft of the New England Patriots who is a truly great manager and thinker and the late Bob Tisch of the New York Giants. Bob was a great businessman who bought the New York Giants against a tide of doubts, and at a low price, and then did a fantastic job. His family is running it well, along with the Mara family. Champions come in all levels in the sports industry, whether in the performance or the business side.

A current champion of note is Tom Brady of the New England Patriots. Tom is one of the great quarterbacks in football history and his golf game isn't too bad either. Tom and I play at my Trump National Golf Club in Westchester and he's not only a champ but a great guy. If he played more golf, he'd be as good as there is. He has amazing talent.

GET IN THE HABIT OF SPEAKING YOUR MIND

Speak like a big thinker. Fear often closes people's mouths when they want to speak. Get in the habit of speaking out in business meetings and social gatherings. Make sure you know what you want to say. Then speak loudly and clearly with the attitude that you have something important to say. Do not be afraid of what other people think. Remember, people are not as smart as you think they are or they think they are.

I fired Kristi Frank in the fifth week of the first season of *The Apprentice* mainly because she didn't speak up. In episode 5, Kristi was in charge of setting up her own bazaar in New York. She did a great job, but the team lost because Omarosa Manigault-Stallworth lost part of the money. Omarosa never took the blame for it. Kristi was blamed for the loss, and never spoke up to defend herself. If she had only spoken up and defended her ability I would have kept her and fired Omarosa instead.

Everyone who does anything is criticized. Expect it. Listen to it. Then dismiss it. I've been criticized for everything I've ever done. I do not let it get to me. Like I said before, everybody goes after the fastest gun in the west. If you're on top you are naturally the target for all those small thinkers who love to criticize big thinkers who make things happen. Do not let it stop you. Speak up and stand out.

At a recent Learning Annex speech the highly respected business writer, Joe Queenan, attended. Joe is known as a tough, no-nonsense kind of guy and he wrote a review in which, in the end, he stated . . . "Trump is a legendary presence, an American financial folk hero who has developed a mysterious rapport with millions of ordinary Americans. . . . What's more, his popularity antedates his success on TV's *The Apprentice*: His brash, go-for-the-throat appeal captured the national imagination more than two decades ago, and has never let go." Joe Queenan concluded that "$30 million or no $30 million, Zanker may have underpaid him."

BIG THINKERS FLOCK TOGETHER

Hang out with other big thinkers. People in your environment have a great impact on you. We're all a product of our environment. Join clubs, associations, and organizations where successful people congregate. Think of yourself as someone important to know. The most important person in any gathering is the one who is most active in introducing him or herself. When meeting a new person look them in the eye and be sure to get their name and give them yours.

Make big thinking friends and meet them regularly for lunch or dinner to trade ideas, voice opinions, and share dreams and aspirations. Be choosy about your friends. Only hang out with people who truly want you to be successful. Drop all your so-called friends who are negative and think small. They will sap your energy. Some may try to block your way and make you feel bad about doing well. Seek advice only from people who know what they're doing.

One of my big thinking friends is John Mack, who heads Morgan Stanley. John is as smart as they come, a totally brilliant Wall Street tactician. He has business vision that is unsurpassed. He is a good friend of mine, and extremely charitable. He heads up the board at New York Hospital.

Recently, John asked me to dinner because there was something he wanted. After beautifully explaining all of the wonderful works being done at New York Hospital (a hospital in which I am not involved, but one of many that would like my involvement, at least financially), John asked me if I could make a contribution of anywhere from 25 to 50 million dollars. I looked at him and said, "Man, do you think big!" Thinking big is one of the reasons that John is so successful.

A short while later, I had lunch with John and presented him with a check for $1 million, which by normal standards is not a small contribution. John was very happy to get it and very gracious, but I've never felt so small or so cheap in handing somebody a $1 million contribution. John does a great job in business and also in helping others that are not so fortunate. He is an incredible example to those reading this book.

BIG ACTION BREEDS BIG CONFIDENCE

Turn your big thoughts into big action as fast as you can. Do not let excuses—"I'm not smart enough," or "I do not have enough experience," or "I'm too young," or "I'm too old," too female or too black, too fat or too thin, too bald, too athletic, or too nerdy, hold you back. These are all just empty excuses. Drop them.

Excuses are a symptom of fear. Plunge in and do the thing you fear the most and your fear will vanish. Nobody is born with confidence. All confidence is acquired. Get the action habit, and your confidence will soar.

Do not spend too much time planning or trying to anticipate and solve problems before they happen. That is just another kind of excuse for procrastination. Until you start, you won't know where the problems will occur. You won't have the experience to solve them. Instead, get into action, and solve the problems as they arise.

Stop thinking and start doing. Start with small things, and take on progressively bigger and bigger challenges to build confidence. That is how Olympic athletes get to the top. They push themselves to bigger and bigger goals, one step at a time.

Actually it is not what you know when you start that matters. It is what you can learn as you go along. When you are starting something new and challenging, always think, "Can do." Your capacity to do anything is simply a state of mind. How much you can do depends on how much you think you can do. Many people get used to working on a certain level of efficiency. When circumstances demand it, they do much more than they think. Start thinking you can do more. Do not build a single-family home, without considering how much more it would cost to construct a multi-unit building or a whole development project. Try to make everything you do bigger, better, and bolder.

Make a commitment to do something big, and you will find a way to do it. I do not mean a vague promise to do something sometime. I mean a legal agreement that puts your feet to the fire. Sign on the dotted line and that will create a fire under your feet that will spur you to move like never before.

Train your mind to accept bigger and bigger goals. Your mind must be ready to take bigger steps. You can't get to a higher level if your mind isn't ready. Let's say you are starting a business that is making $100 a month and you want to get to $10,000 a month. Most people can't shoot from $100 to $10,000 overnight. Your mind needs to adjust to the idea. Start with smaller steps to get your mind ready and to build bridges from where you are now to where you want to be.

It helps to get a mentor to help you jump to a higher level faster. That is why there are master teachers and coaches in every field. For some reason we're all receptive to advice we receive from authority figures. Find an authority figure in your field and get his or her advice and encouragement to take bigger and bolder steps. Their confidence helps to boost your confidence.

USE LEVERAGE TO EXTRACT TOP DOLLAR FOR YOUR WORK

Thinking big is the leverage you need to get paid what you are worth. In the real world people are not going to just hand you money. People fight and kill for money. In the make-believe world you will automatically get paid what you are worth. The real world doesn't work that way. You get paid what you are worth only when the person you are dealing with has no other choice.

Doctors get paid a lot because you pay or you die. Dentists get paid a lot because you pay or he leaves you with an aching tooth. Lawyers get a big commission or they kill your deal. There is an old saying, "No pain, no gain." It usually applies to bodybuilding, but it works for negotiations as well. Superstar athletes can demand high salaries and hefty signing bonuses because professional teams need them.

Movie stars can demand a huge piece of the action because

the movie companies need them to attract audiences. It is the same for top coaches, supernova models, and rock stars. They demand high incomes because if you do not pay them they walk straight to your competitors and you lose. It is a form of legal bribery. That is exactly how lawyers get so rich.

To be super successful you have to use leverage to extract top dollar for what you do. You've got to threaten to inflict some pain before you get some gain. In every successful real estate deal I have had to make my opponent feel the pain of what he would lose if he did not do the deal with me, and the pleasure of going forward on the deal and giving me what I want.

Everybody knows this, but few people talk about it. Look at job negotiations. Most people get their biggest raises when they change jobs, or threaten to change jobs. When negotiating for more money, build up the value of your presence to the company, and increase the loss the company will suffer in losing you. Always be prepared to walk. Use the leverage of the threat of leaving to get a bigger raise.

HOOK YOUR CAREER TO A BIG TREND

Take advantage of big trends. Many events that occur appear surprising to most people but are really quite inevitable and predictable. Look below the surface of the quickly changing daily news to the big sweeping changes that take decades to play out. That is where you can find big ideas. There are demographic, cultural, financial, technological, and medical trends in place now that will produce predictable results years from now. There are shortages of doctors and nurses, and at the same time the population is aging rapidly. There is a growing Hispanic population, a migration out of the suburbs to the far suburbs, called the exurbs, a growth in the number of single people, and a cultural shift in people thinking more ecologically.

There are huge opportunities for profits if you can think big and create big solutions for the human needs brought about by trends. Although I am one of the world's biggest developers, I saw great potential in Jersey City. I am good at predicting trends and I see a good future in Jersey City. That is why I built Trump Plaza Jersey City, a $415 million condominium project that will include two towers, over 50 stories high, with 862 luxury condominiums. I also chose a great partner, Dean Geibel, who made it happen!

DO NOT STALL OUT
HALFWAY TO THE TOP

Do not get stuck in a halfway successful rut. Some people start out with big goals. They start out thinking big, and it works. They achieve a level of success, a good job, money in the bank, a nice income, a retirement plan, and some play toys like a boat or a luxury car. Then they stop thinking big, and start thinking about playing it safe and protecting what they have. Do not fall into that trap.

Keep stimulating your mind with big ideas. Be a collector of big ideas. Constantly fill your mind with new information, and use this new information to spawn new ideas. Put these ideas together to create big ideas for solving problems, making money, getting things done faster and cheaper, and making complex things simple.

SET THE BAR EVER HIGHER

Always strive to outdo yourself, setting the bar higher and higher. When I was building the Trump Tower, I didn't want just another skyscraper, I wanted to create a skyscraper like none that had ever been built before. I wanted to use a bold beautiful innovative glass and bronze exterior that would put the Trump Tower in a class of its own. Some people advised me to hang beautiful paintings in the Trump Tower lobby. That seemed unoriginal and boring to me. I wanted something absolutely breathtaking and spectacular that had never been seen before in Manhattan. In 1980 I spent 2 million dollars to build an 80-foot waterfall in the Trump Tower lobby, and it has become a major tourist attraction for visitors to New York City.

After the Trump Tower was completed, I knew I wanted more, an even greater challenge, so I built many great buildings and developments. Recently I built Trump World Tower at the United Nations Plaza. This ninety-story skyscraper is the world's tallest residential building and the world's forty-eighth tallest building. It has been a spectacular success, and it is an example of what you can do when you try to outdo your best. I am now topping it in Chicago with a ninety-two-story building in Chicago's best location.

BIG VISIONS OF WHAT CAN BE

When faced with a big challenge, do not look at what is, instead focus on what can be. When I purchased 40 Wall Street, everyone else saw a huge building that would be an enormous cash drain. I saw an opportunity to pick up a prime piece of real estate, a landmark building for a fraction of its value. I saw what it could become. What I saw was worth much more than the price. I did the same thing with the Mar-a-Lago Club in Palm Beach. Before I came along this huge house was a white elephant that nobody would buy because nobody would feel comfortable living in a 128-room monstrosity sitting on the ocean. I envisioned an exclusive club that would assign a high value on the experience of socializing in such opulent surroundings.

Columbia University had a great opportunity to build one of the finest and most spectacular campuses anywhere in the world. One of the most successful businessmen in the United States named Al Lerner, who also owned the Cleveland Browns Football Team, was on the board of Columbia and wanted to buy a portion of a huge development I was involved in on the West Side of Manhattan. It would have given Columbia large acreage, fronting on the Hudson River between 59th and 62nd Street directly behind Lincoln Center. It was his vision to build Columbia's Business School and School of Performing Arts there, and what a vision it would have been.

The deal was very close to being done when all of a sudden Al called and said, "Donald, I've just been diagnosed with cancer. I won't be alive for very long." It is amazing what sickness does, even when you have a cold deals no longer matter, but in Al's case he had far worse than that. He was a strong, tough, but wonderful guy with a brilliant vision. It was that vision and tenaciousness that built his business.

In any event, Al passed away and the new President of Columbia, Lee Bollinger, who came from the University of Michigan, didn't like the idea. Instead, he wanted to build Columbia's new buildings in a lousy location on land that, in certain instances, the school did not even own. Once the project was announced, it became virtually impossible to acquire the holdings because everybody wanted top dollar. He actually announced his project before buying the land—dummy!

In any event, Columbia Prime was a great idea thought of by a great man that ultimately fizzled due to poor leadership at Columbia. Just like the University of Michigan was lucky to get rid of Bollinger, so will Columbia—someday in the future!

BE PREPARED FOR BIG SETBACKS

Realize that big thinking sometimes means big setbacks. In life there is no success without hardship. Everyone suffers setbacks. It is part of life. If you think big you will encounter big setbacks from time to time. What really matters is how you respond to them. Every great artist, doctor, lawyer, scientist, inventor, athlete, musician, politician, real estate developer, corporate executive, entrepreneur, and salesman uses failure to his or her advantage. The greats in every field got to be great by learning from failure. They analyze their failures and discover inventive new ways of succeeding.

A failure or setback is not a defeat. Defeat is a state of mind. You are defeated only when you accept defeat, and assume the hopeless mind-set of a defeated person. Learn from your mistakes and view your setbacks as the cost of getting an education. It is very healthy to engage in some constructive self-criticism. It helps you become a better person. Never accept defeat. Never overcriticize yourself. Never let a setback defeat you emotionally to the point that you draw negative self-deprecating conclusions like, "I'll never make it. I'm a loser. I might as well give up. All my critics were right."

That is the point at which self-criticism is unhealthy and dangerous. Do not do it. For it could ruin your entire life. When I went through my setbacks of the 1990s I saw lots of my friends give in to self-criticism that was so powerful they never recovered. It killed their spirit. They were never heard from again. Some people actually commit suicide because the pain of self-recrimination is so bad.

Do not view any failure as the end. Learn your lessons

quickly, then move on. Do not dwell on the failure. Start thinking big again. Fill your mind with thoughts that make you feel good, plans for the future, past successes, good things your friends have said about you, anything that puts a positive spin on your inner dialogue.

Learn the art of forgetting. Move on and do not give a thought to the bad things that have happened to you. Do not be an idealist, wishing things were different, wishing bad things had never happened, and wishing you lived in a fairy tale world where everything always turns out right. Do not wait for everything to be perfect before you start taking action again. Be a realist. It will never be perfect. Just resolve to do better, then move on, forgetting the past. View every failure as a step on the way to ultimate success. Remember, persistence plus learning from mistakes equals success.

Think big, but keep your feet on the ground and your fingers on the till. You've got to know what you can do. There are always forces at work that can bring you down, jealous bureaucrats, greedy lawyers, cheating contractors, weak-kneed bankers. Do not get so caught up in your big dreams and daring ideas that you forget about the basics. You need to always remember to provide above all a quality product, and make sure you have the safeguards in place to make sure you get paid. Think big, but take care of the basics.

ZANKER'S TAKE

I started The Learning Annex twenty-eight years ago in my tiny New York City studio apartment. I had to start it on the cheap, using only my $5,000 bar mitzvah money as seed capital. I always tried to make us look bigger than we were. I gave the building superintendent a few bucks to allow me to put up an extra sign on the janitor's closet door in the hallway next to my real entrance: "The Learning Annex—Enter Room 101" with an arrow pointing to my door. It made it look like my offices were twice as big as they really were. Then I made my studio look more like an office by folding the bed into the couch every day.

We were growing and needed more space. We didn't have the cash to rent another room. I had to improvise to find ways to make a bigger splash with small capital. So I found a woman who agreed to rent me her dining room table, in her apartment upstairs from me, to use as a "cubicle" during the day while she was working. I had a Learning Annex phone extension installed in her apartment with a huge plug that allowed five employees to work off the one line. But she had only agreed to let one person use the room. Every night I made sure I got the five workers out of the apartment exactly at 6 P.M. before she arrived home from work and saw them all there.

In the early days Tony Robbins taught me a lot about ratcheting up my energy to a higher intensity. You can't help being intense when you spend time around Tony Robbins. He's a human dynamo! I learned my first lessons in thinking big from Tony. In the 1980s my attitude of thinking big was responsible for putting The Learning Annex on the map.

One of the things I did to create a feeling of being very wealthy was to wear a very expensive suit. I always wore a $1,000 suit even if I had little money. So instead of buying ten cheap suits, I bought one extremely expensive suit, which I wore to all my important business meetings. I called it, "Le Suit."

It made me feel great, very important and very rich. It attracted people. And although nobody would say anything out loud to my face, everyone knew I was dressed like a very rich man. In a subtle way, everyone I met felt a little bit better about me because of that $1,000 suit. Each year all my office managers would come to New York to meet for our company retreat. I would take them all to the Armani shop, and each one would have to buy a $1,000 Armani suit, both the men and the women. I wouldn't let anyone buy a suit for $750. That was too cheap. It had to be $1,000 or more. That was the 80s. Now we all buy $3,000 suits.

Another thing I did was to carry $5,000 in cash in my pocket whenever I went to important business meetings with high level people. I would walk into an office or meet for lunch or dinner dressed in my $1,000 Armani suit, carrying $5,000 cash in my pocket. Carrying all this money put a spring in my step. I wouldn't carry it to spend. It is all in the attitude. I felt very rich, and the other person would sense this immediately. They'd think, "This guy's a winner."

I'd carry the $5,000 even if that was the last $5,000 in my account. I'd draw it all out and carry it with me to the meeting. Now I carry $10,000 to important meetings. And for every big meeting, like my meetings with Donald

Trump, I carry $15,000 in cash in my pockets! It feels good and attracts the right people and the right deals. It makes me remember I am rich.

After meeting Donald Trump I got a whole new idea of what it is to think big. I realized that what I considered thinking big was actually thinking very small in Donald Trump's world. Dealing with him forced me to think ten times bigger than I had ever thought before. It took a lot of courage to take this giant leap. But I am glad I did, because in the three years since meeting Donald Trump my business has grown twenty times bigger than it was before.

Donald Trump has the attitude that anything is possible. He doesn't let any deal or possibility, however huge, intimidate him. It boils down to this: If a worthy goal comes his way that he wants to achieve he'll achieve it. He never lets fear of failure stop him from something he wants to do. Since meeting Donald I have made a conscious effort to meet more people of his caliber. And I've found that they all have the same think big attitude.

In November 2005 media mogul Rupert Murdoch auctioned off a one-hour lunch with himself on eBay, with the proceeds to benefit the Jerusalem College of Technology. My $57,100 bid beat all the other bidders and I won the privilege of having a one-hour lunch with him in New York City. It was a small price to pay for the opportunity to break bread with Rupert Murdoch. I took the opportunity to talk to him about the best ways in his opinion to expand The Learning Annex. He displayed the same no-holds-barred mentality that Donald Trump has. It was worth paying Rupert Murdoch $1,000 a minute for a lunch. It feels like a bargain compared to what I am paying Donald Trump.

Warren Buffett is America's second richest man. I wanted to invite him to teach at the Wealth Expos. So when I heard that he put his car up for sale on the Internet, I got very interested. If mine was the winning bid the money would go to his favorite charity, Girls, Inc., and he would pick me up in the car in a chauffeur's cap. It would be a great opportunity to meet the legendary stock market expert, and ask him to teach a class on "How You Can Invest at Any Age."

I won the auction and paid Warren Buffett $73,200 for his used Lincoln Town Car. Then I offered him $2 million to speak at the Expo. He didn't accept the offer, but it was an extraordinary experience that gave me a glimpse into the character of this amazingly successful human being.

I spent all this money to meet with Rupert Murdoch and Warren Buffett. And what did I learn? I learned that Rupert, Warren, and Donald all have the attitude of thinking big and kicking ass. Adopt this big attitude and you'll be unstoppable.

TO SUM IT UP

No matter what you do, think big. Thinking big is the driving force that has forged all the great achievements in modern life, from the towering skyscrapers to the amazing discoveries in science, technology, and medicine, to the great industrial and military achievements. Thinking big is what creates loving and lasting relationships. Simply take a big goal and mold yourself to become the person who can accomplish that goal. Most people are afraid to think big. They can't imagine themselves doing big things because they do not have the knowledge, the experience, the track record. You do not need these things to think big. You can start thinking big without all the trappings of success. Every big thinker has had to start as a nobody. Just think big and that immediately distinguishes you from the vast majority of people. How big you think determines how big a success you become. Everything else is secondary.

KEY POINTS

- Thinking big has led to all of humankind's greatest achievements.
- Focus on the top and you will get there.
- It is easier to do things on a large scale.
- Overcome the fear of thinking big.
- Mold yourself into the person who can do big things.
- Adopt a big attitude to go with your big thinking.
- Give yourself a big definition.
- Draw positive conclusions about yourself.
- Go first class all the way.
- Display a big attitude in your personal and social life as well.
- Always think of yourself as someone who is important.
- Speak out like a big thinker.
- Hang out with other big thinkers.
- Put big thoughts into action right away.
- Build confidence starting with small successes that lead to greater and greater successes.
- Take advantage of big trends.
- Keep away from negative people in business and life.
- Avoid sinking into dangerous self-criticism.
- After every setback, start thinking big as soon as possible.

APPENDIX

FREQUENTLY ASKED QUESTIONS

THE BEST OF DONALD'S QUESTION

AND ANSWER SESSIONS FROM THE LEARNING

ANNEX WEALTH EXPOS IN NORTH AMERICA

1. Q: *When you hire your employees, what exact qualities do you look for?*

DT: I like to hire people that I know. That is why I love to promote from within. A lot of times, I'll see people on the other side of the deal that I'm really impressed with because they are extremely tough negotiators. So I hire them.

It's dangerous to hire people you don't know. You put an ad in *The New York Times*. A guy walks into your office, he looks good, he sounds good, and then he turns out to be a stiff. I like to hire people that I've had a chance to see under fire.

2. Q: *I came here from Russia, and I love this country very much. Since the Democrats have taken over the Senate and the House, do you think the real estate market will get better?*

DT: You never know. Real estate is so dependent on interest rates. Now, with all of the money that we're spending on wars that we shouldn't be in and lots of other useless things, it's going to be hard to keep rates down. If rates stay low, real estate will be great. If rates go up appreciably, real estate will be in trouble. It's very simple, in my opinion.

3. Q: *My partner and I have $10 million to invest. We want to know what market you would recommend and what type of project in today's climate?*

DT: A great place to invest right now in New York City is Harlem. It's starting to really go up. Harlem is actually one of the hottest places in real estate. It makes sense. We're all on this little island, surrounded by water. Property is limited. I know a lot of friends who are doing very well in Harlem.

4. **Q:** *Mr. Trump, since you are not running for president, who do we support and how do we get started?*

DT: You have a lot of good people. Rudy Giuliani is a very good person. Hillary Clinton is a very good person. We might not like what's going on right now, but we live in a very resilient country, and we'll find a way out of our problems. This country is very, very resilient.

5. **Q:** *Why do you think it's so important to give back?*

DT: I think it's very important. I just gave almost five hundred acres to create a park in Westchester and Putnam counties in New York. I feel good about it. It's the right thing to do. When you make a lot of money, you owe it to give back. It makes you feel good. It makes me feel good, and it comes back!

6. **Q:** *What is the passion that keeps you going?*

DT: I just love what I'm doing, I love it. That's all it is, very simple. In the end, you kick the bucket, nobody cares, but you know why I do it? Because I have fun doing it. I love building buildings and it keeps me happy.

7. Q: *I'm trying to build a team for my company. What are the key things you would look for when hiring?*

DT: Well, the thing that's most important to me is loyalty. You can't hire loyalty. I've had people over the years who I swore were loyal to me, and it turned out that they weren't. Then I've had people that I didn't have the same confidence in and turned out to be extremely loyal. So you never really know. The thing I really look for though, over the longer term, is loyalty.

8. Q: *I'm thinking big. I'm taking your advice. If people don't increase their financial education, what do you see happening to America, to our world?*

DT: Well, it's very tough to be successful without knowledge. You need knowledge. However, now you can get lucky, or you can get a really good job. I know a lot of guys who didn't go to high school, and they are tremendous success stories. It's very hard, and it's a very unique and rare person to become very successful without knowledge. So you should try obtaining all the knowledge you can get. Whether you go to college or whether you teach yourself by reading books, you should try to get every ounce of knowledge you can. Then you are going to have a much better chance.

9. Q: *I watch your show,* The Apprentice *all the time, and I absolutely love it. I noticed that you always manage to get very beautiful women on your show. In your opinion which woman is the hottest?*

DT: There was one woman on *The Apprentice* who I thought was absolutely beautiful. I won't say who she was. When I saw her, I said she's going to be a star. This woman is going to be a star, she's so beautiful. You know what? She wasn't. She fizzled out. She didn't have the inner something to fight to get to the top no matter what it took. In other words, she was beautiful, and I don't want to insult her by saying this, but she didn't have the inner fire to make it really big.

It happens with both men and women. A lot of times a man or a woman will be very handsome or beautiful. They've had it so easy in life that when it comes time to competing with people that have had to work a lot harder than them, they don't have the fire in the belly that it takes to succeed. I've seen really beautiful people that were total stiffs.

10. Q: *Would you ever consider owning a professional sports team again?*

DT: I would, but I'd much rather watch Bob Kraft continue to win. I love him. He's a great man and he has done an amazing job with the New England Patriots. I think that Tom Brady is a winner.

11. Q: *Did you think big when you were a teenager, or is this something that developed over time?*

DT: I always thought big. I always wanted to get out of Queens. Not that Queens was bad; it's good. I always wanted to come to Manhattan.

12. Q: *If you had $25,000 what would you invest it in?*

DT: That's always a tough question, because I don't know what your abilities are, okay? I hate to say the stock market, because that's just a crap shoot. I would go out and buy some property in areas that you think are going to get better. I'd go borrow some money. I'd fix it up and sell it for a profit. You do that five or ten times, all of a sudden you have a nice nest egg, then you go into bigger deals.

13. Q: *I own my own business and my business partner is stealing my company away from me.*

DT: You go and get yourself the meanest, most vicious lawyer you can find and a good accountant and just make his life miserable. You might have to do a contingent deal. Go see ten lawyers and pick the one you think is the best and the one you can make the best deal with. Go after that bastard. Don't let him take advantage of you.

14. Q: *What's a good golf tip?*

DT: A good golf tip, just try and swing nice and easy and pretend it doesn't matter. That's true in life, by the way.

15. Q: *I recently heard that a prenup that was videotaped has never been broken.*

DT: That's right. It's important because a lot of times, the other spouse will say they were forced to do it, or they didn't know what they were doing. When you put it on tape, you can prove they knew what they were signing. This way the judge can see the entire ceremony. You need a pre-nup, but it's horrible to say to someone you love, "I love you, darling, I love you very much. You are the apple of my eye. We're going to be married forever, but just in case it doesn't work out, sign this freakin' document."

16. **Q:** *I'm 16-years-old, and I just want to know at what age you first made an investment?*

DT: Well I did investments very early, from the time I was in college. I'd buy little town houses in not-so-great neighborhoods in Philadelphia. I'd fix them and flip them. I think it's a great thing to do when you're starting out. After you do a couple the banks like you. Remember one thing, the banks need you more than you need them. There are always banks around that want to loan you money to buy property. People who own town houses, will take back mortgages, because they can't sell. As a buyer you're coming into a very good real estate market because you can make some pretty good deals now. I love to buy little things, fix them up, sell them for a profit, and then do it again and again and again. Do it with certain banks, create a track record and you are going to do fine. Just do it.

17. **Q:** *If you had $50,000 would you invest it in residential or commercial real estate?*

DT: Today I would invest it in residential, but I'd really want a good deal and I'd use it and leverage up, because with $50,000 you can borrow probably $500,000. I'd buy something really, really great, but I'd go in and negotiate like crazy. I wouldn't spend the whole $50,000 either, by the way.

18. **Q:** *You've been married to the most beautiful women in the world. Do you have a secret or a special pickup line?*

DT: That's a hell of a question. I'd agree. They are all beautiful. I actually get along with all of them too, which is hard to do. I don't have a secret. Chemistry is an amazing thing. I could be with a group of people and I would have chemistry with some, but I wouldn't have chemistry with others. I think the big thing is you have to find somebody that you have chemistry with. Prior to my marriage, I would go out with a woman that was very beautiful, but if there was no chemistry, no matter what I did, then it just wasn't going to work. So you have to find somebody you can get along with, that you'd be friends with, and that you have great chemistry with. What the hell do I know, I've been divorced twice?

19. Q: *How do you run a successful business and be a good father at the same time?*

DT: Oftentimes, with success you will hurt your family life. Now if you are married to a person that wants you to be successful and is proud of your success, then you are more likely to be successful in both your business and your marriage.

A friend of mine was a very hard worker and was really moving up in one of the biggest Wall Street firms. His wife was constantly bickering and complaining that he worked too hard and that he was away on weekends. This guy was not away weekends cheating on his wife. He was a hard worker. He loved his wife, but she just broke his ass.

Once I called her and said, "This guy is really moving up in the company and he's doing a great job. Instead of coming down on him like you do all the time, why don't you encourage him? He's doing a terrific job. He's making a lot of money and that's going to be good for you and the kids." She said, "Well he's never home. He's never home during the weekends, blah, blah, blah." I said, "He's never home? He's home 85 percent of the time. The other 15 percent of the time he's away. If you keep this up you are going to lose him, because he's not going to be able to take it, and he's going to have to make a choice."

Eventually he got rid of her. He met a woman that gives him a lot of great encouragement. Now he's the happiest guy in the world. He works even harder and he doesn't feel guilty. She's so proud of him. This goes for the husband and the wife. You have to encourage each other and if you don't, in my opinion, the marriage is never going to work out.

20. **Q:** *What do you think about the relationship between the United States and Cuba?*

DT: That's a very dangerous question. Every country in the world is in Cuba right now, except the United States. Castro is old and sick. I looked at him the other day on television. I said, "Man, that guy is tough. He doesn't die!" Cuba's going to be an amazing story in the coming years. I think it's about time we start thinking a little bit differently about Cuba, because certainly every other country in the world is.

21. **Q:** *I had three foreclosures because of poor investment choices. After foreclosure and the bank takes the property back, for what amount of time can the bank come after you?*

DT: That's too bad. That's a legal question. Every state is different. Generally, they can't come after you at all if you have not guaranteed the mortgage personally. You can try to negotiate a deal with the bank, rather than allowing the banks to take those buildings. In many cases you can go see the bankers and cut a deal to reduce the interest or the principal. Maybe they'll carry the principal to a later date.

If the banks are stuck with these houses, then it doesn't make sense for them to foreclose. I'd say, "Look fellas, you're going to take my house away. I'm a good guy. I make money. I want to pay you. I'm going to pay whatever everyone else is going to pay. No one else is going to give you back the money anyway." They're likely to cut a deal, because otherwise they are going to have a nonperforming loan on their books. They are going to have to put the house up for auction. They will be getting far less than what you are going to pay and the bank is probably not going to be able to sell it very easily.

Now it's tougher if you bought the property two or three years ago, when everybody was getting those floating mortgages where your payment goes up when the interest rates go up. I begged people three years ago at The Learning Annex Wealth Expos, not to do those mortgages. Those mortgages were a disaster. It's hard not to go for these mortgages. You have a very low rate of interest and you can afford to pay a little bit more for the property. You think you're going to always earn a big enough income to make the payments even if the interest does go up.

You see what's happening now. These mortgages are exploding and the rates are going through the roof. I've had many people write me and thank me for telling them not to do it years ago. I'm very happy about it. If you are going to lose your house, go in and negotiate with the bank. I think you can make a deal.

22. **Q:** *What is the hottest time to buy real estate, in your opinion, or does it matter?*

DT: Right now! I don't want to buy in a hot market. I want to go into a dead shit market. This is the time to start thinking about buying. I really made a lot of money. I really understand real estate, especially when I'm focused, which is another point, being focused. Stay focused, good times or bad, stay focused. Don't think you're so hot. Stay focused. This is now a great time. You also have to find a great location. You could be a really smart person, but if you are in a location that's going nowhere over the next thirty years, then you know what, you are wasting your time. I don't understand why people don't pick up from bad locations and move to good locations and then start buying. Where is a very, very good question. San Francisco is a good location. Start looking at buying real estate at discounted prices there right now.

23. **Q:** *I'm a real estate broker here in South Florida. I have a lot of listings, and I want to know what to say to my sellers?*

DT: Three years ago those sellers were in a position of strength and back then you used to ask, what do I tell my buyers, Mr. Trump? This is the time to buy real estate and get a good deal. I don't mean somebody puts a price of a million dollars, and you say, "I'll take it." I mean, you offer half of a million dollars. This is the time to negotiate.

I feel very guilty. I built a job in Westchester, and I sold the units for an average of $2 million. It's a beautiful job. That was three years ago at the height of the market.

I got lucky. I sold these units at the top of the market. Now there are three of them for sale. I'm offering them $1.2 million. I want to buy them back. Then I'll sell them in two years for a profit. It's a game, then you die and nobody cares. It's over. We all play games, but I feel guilty. They bought it for $2 million, I offered them $1.2 million. I won't get it for $1.2 million, but I'll get them for $1.5 and rent them for two years. This is the time to make these kinds of deals.

24. Q: *What's more exciting for you, the chase of the deal or the close of the deal?*

DT: Well the chase and the close are the same. Really the question is the chase or long-term owning. I love the chase. The chase is always fun and exciting, but you have to do something with the chase. When the chase is over you've got to get down to business and make something work. A lot of people that do well with the chase aren't good managers, because it's a different ability. The great managers aren't usually the good hunters and it's rare that you find somebody that's good as a hunter and then can do something with it.

25. Q: *A good friend of mine said, smart people learn from their mistakes, smarter people learn from others. I'm here to learn from you.*

DT: You can learn from both. You are going to make mistakes, everybody is going to make mistakes. If I took the most successful people in the room, they'll tell me they made some big mistakes. The key to mistakes is not letting the mistake bring you down. I have a friend, who for twenty-five years was a tremendous success. He bought a little company, he bought another, and another. He bought like 412 companies. Then he bet the entire ranch on one deal that was bigger than his company and the deal was a stinker. He got screwed by Wall Street, and it brought his company down.

So you want to learn from your mistakes, but you also want to learn from other people's mistakes. No matter how good you are there will be mistakes. I know every really smart New York killer. I know every deal-maker in New York. They are either friends or enemies, but I know them all. I can name, for each one of them, deals that were made that were bad. You've got to learn from them.

26. **Q:** *I'm a young woman with an entrepreneurial mind. What advice would you give to me, go to college or start in the real estate business?*

DT: I would say, there is nothing like education. You can put it down and I can give you lots of examples of people that didn't need education to get ahead in life. When you get a college degree it's like a card that says, "This person has accomplished something." It opens a lot of doors for you.

27. **Q:** *While you were growing up what was the best advice that your mom and dad gave you?*

DT: They gave me different advice. My mother was a wife who really was a great homemaker. She always said, "Be happy!" She wanted me to be happy. My father understood me more and he said, "I want you to be successful." He was a very driven kind of a guy. That's why I'm so screwed up, because I had a father that pushed me pretty hard. My father was a tough man, but he was a good man. He was a kind man, and he would tell me to always do something that you love. Now I'm happy. So I ended up doing what both of my parents wanted me to do.

28. **Q:** *What do you see as the solution for the energy crisis?*

DT: We could make energy with solar or wave technology. I don't like the wind so much, because it's really not efficient. I'm building this big facility at Jones Beach, New York. They want to put four hundred windmills on the horizon. I think it's a terrible idea. There are so many different

forms of energy that we could be totally energy independent in a very short period of time. I hate to tell you this,
but if you look at the smart countries that are doing very
well, the energy form they are going to is nuclear energy.
There's no reason for us to be buying oil for $70 and $80 a
barrel. There are so many different ways to solve that problem. Real estate's great, oil is great, but energy and alternative forms of energy are a great business for you to get into,
in my opinion.

29. **Q:** *The biggest business regret?*

DT: I feel a little bit sorry sometimes that I did a deal, but I
don't have regrets. You have to learn from your mistakes
because we all make them. I can take the greatest deal-
makers in the world, and they all made bad deals. They
made mostly good deals, but they made bad deals too. The
key to making a bad deal is it shouldn't be a deal that takes
you down. It shouldn't be a deal that destroys you. That is
the key. I made some bad deals, but I learned from them
and they never took me down.

30. Q: *Do you think people should pay off their mortgages or take that money out and invest it?*

DT: In good times I love to be heavy in borrowing, nothing smarter than when you are borrowed up to the hilt in good times. Then bad times come, then you can get crushed. It depends on your mortgage, it depends on whether you have a fixed rate going out to thirty years at an interest rate you can handle or if you have a floating rate mortgage. I wouldn't pay off a thirty-year fixed mortgage with a good rate. If you have a good rate, keep it. If you are being crushed because your interests are floating way the hell up, I would try and get rid of that sucker real fast.

31. Q: *You have been very successful in branding several of your products like the Trump clothing line. What else are you coming up with and when are you going to bring out the best Trump coffee?*

DT: My main thing is real estate. I love the suits, I love the ties, I love the shirts, but my big thing is real estate. I'm building buildings all over the world now. We have seventy-two different jobs. I'm building all over the world and that's the thing I love the most. The branding is important for real estate, because people know when they are buying one of my buildings, it is a great building. I'm all about quality. It doesn't always have to be the highest building, but it has to be the best quality building. I'm all about quality. When I build a building people know they are getting a great location. I sell buildings out and some people don't even get to see the building, because they have confidence in my brand. So brand is very, very important.

32. **Q:** *I think you are such a great builder, and I really admire you for that, because there is a sense of beauty in your buildings, especially Trump Tower. My question is, how could you put together projects on schedule when you have so many in different places, and then how do you attract really good tenants?*

DT: Well to a certain extent, we're all subject to being victims of the market. When the market's good it's a lot easier to get those tenants. I always find that if you get the right product, in the right location, and get it built and have the right pricing, it will get rented. Lots of good things will happen. I've felt that very, very strongly, from the beginning. Trump Tower is an example. It's been a successful building from the day I built it and it opened in 1982.

It's been a successful building because people love the building.

33. **Q:** *What is it that resides in your personal tools that created the burning desire to make money?*

DT: I don't have a burning desire to make money. I have a burning desire to enjoy what I do. I make a lot of money because I enjoy what I do and I do it well. I don't have this burning desire. It's never a money thing. I love building buildings, I love doing real estate, I love doing *The Apprentice*. I love doing the things that I do. They make money, because I'm good at it.

34. **Q:** *What advice do you have for someone who wants to get started in commercial real estate development?*

DT: What you really have to do for a period of a year or two is get yourself a job with one of the good firms in town. Then after that, you'll decide, do I stay or do I go out on my own? That's going to be your decision and that's going to be a very tough decision to make.

35. Q: *I am finalizing a contract on a commercial property and we have discussed the terms and we are trying to finish it. How do I get the seller to stick with what he's told me and put it on paper?*

DT: It's actually a good question. Sometimes you have to have the ability to take a walk. In other words he's renegotiating with you right? Sometimes you have to be able to get up and say, you've cheated me, you've lied to me, you've misrepresented to me, I'm leaving. Now, one of two things is going to happen. You are going to blow the deal or you are going to get everything you want. If you are not prepared to do it, don't do it. You have to always have the ability to walk.

That's why I do so many deals. I always like to be able to walk away from certain deals and take the best ones. I work on ten deals at a time. I have a friend, he's worked on one deal for two years and it still isn't done. He's given up a big portion of his life for one deal. I say to him, "You can't negotiate, because these guys have you. You've too much of your own capital and energy tied up in this one deal."

36. Q: *What do you think about the green building? Is it a fad or is it actually the future?*

DT: I'm doing one right now. I'm doing this huge complex in Jones Beach in coordination with the State of New York. It's on the ocean and it's going to be great. I made a deal to build a regular building and all of a sudden the state wants me to do a green building. I could have challenged them, because I have my long-term lease. A new commissioner came in and just wanted a green building. It's much more expensive. The science has not been perfected yet and in some cases the savings cannot justify the huge cost. You spend a tremendous amount of money now, and it takes forty years to get your money back.

Even with the tax breaks it doesn't work financially. For example, if I use solar, I get my money back with the tax breaks in twelve years. I've made better deals than that, folks. It's not the greatest.

Green is getting better, and it's starting to happen. I think they can make cars that would take virtually no gasoline, and we could wipe out some of the problems that we have. I don't know why they are not doing it. It's a very hard thing to justify in terms of real estate right now. It's a long, long time before you get your money back. I think that will get better with technology.

37. **Q:** *Being so busy, how did you make your children so suc-cessful? How did you prevent them from getting into bad habits? What is your advice to parents to help them make their children successful other than just putting them in a good school?*

DT: My children seem to be doing well. You don't know. Life is so fragile, folks, you don't know exactly what's going on. They might do well today and tomorrow I'll get home and I'll say, how are you doing, and there's a problem. I was very strict with my children. I raised them very tough. I didn't throw money at them. They weren't very spoiled. They were just naturally smart and they were good stu-dents. You really have to let them know that life isn't all about the private jets and about the big houses. So far they are very industrious and very hard working. I'm probably getting more credit from my kids than I have for a lot of other things.

TESTIMONIALS

Dear Mr. Trump,

Last weekend my husband and I attended the Real Estate Expo in Toronto. We live in Ypsilanti, Michigan, the town right next to Ann Arbor. Currently we own 7 million dollars worth of real estate and have been negotiating a Purchase Agreement for the past 4 months on an 8 million dollar shopping center. We have read every one of your books and want to let you know that whenever we are negotiating, looking at real estate, dealing with contractors or tenants and we're not sure of an answer, we always say "What would Trump do?" Those four little words along with the knowledge derived from your books has helped us build our business and is part of the reason why we are successful. In the real estate business there are so many people that not only don't help, they try and sabotage and I am thankful that you write books, sharing your experience and knowledge which has helped us attain our dreams.

After the weekend seminar, listening to you, Tony Robbins, George Foreman and the rest of the speakers we feel like we are unstoppable and we have the next 25 years to work. As you are aware, Michigan's economy is terrible and we feel like kids in a candy store because there are so many deals it is hard to choose. We returned from Toronto Monday afternoon and already are looking at two new commercial properties to acquire. Thank you for spending three hours with us in Toronto. You have truly made a difference in our lives.

Sincerely,

Karen Maurer
Eric Maurer

Thinking BIG

I attended The Learning Annex Wealth Expo in Philadelphia in April of 2007. Having grown tired of twenty-five years in the corporate world, I knew I needed to make a change. I have several friends in the Commercial Real Estate business who have done very well for themselves and I knew that this is what I wanted to be involved in, but I just did not know where to start. Corporate life was really beginning to suck the life out of me.

I listened attentively to Donald Trump. He spoke of all of his successes and even mentioned some of his failures. My biggest fear in making a change was the fear of failure. But what I learned from Mr. Trump, was that if you don't take a chance and take a calculated risk, you can never succeed. I have since left my corporate job and I am excited about a new consulting opportunity before me. The Learning Annex Wealth Expo and Donald Trump have really made a difference in my life and have given me the courage to go out on my own. All I can say is "Thank You."

Sincerely,

Steven Martino

Thanks for the advice!

The absolute best advice I have employed so far in my real estate career was when Mr. Trump advised to make very low initial offers on property. He said that it will sometimes bring out the truth of what the person believes their property is actually worth and/or it will plant the seed that it is not quite worth as much as they are asking (which could also work in your favor). Well, I grabbed this gem and use it as often as I can. Recently, I had a client that was willing to pay list price for a home they really loved. I convinced them to make an initial offer 25 percent below asking price! They were very scared, but agreed. The seller was desperate and didn't meet our offer, but came way down on the very first counter. My client accepted it and was thrilled, as they were ready to pay list! This is a phenomenal technique that takes some guts to try, but you don't become a Donald Trump without guts!

Respectfully,

Carl C. Anderson

Thank you, Donald!

I literally hit the bottom of the barrel, carved my name on the bottom and rose up stronger than ever in less than two years! Thanks to Donald Trump, I now understand that I have the power to create what I want to achieve in my mind, and that whatever I can conceive in my mind I can manifest in the physical world as well. This is why Donald's words are so profound when he says to think big because you have to go there in your mind thousands of times before you can bring it about physically. I have become a Producer and a true Capitalist, with power to create my own universe as I go along. Thank You!

Warmest Regards,

Wayne M. Aston, Founder and CEO Aztec Holdings Inc., Co-Founder, Celerity Investments, Celaritas Realty, Celerity Property Management, Celerity Development Incorporated

---

TRUMP's Kick-Ass Attitude!

I saw and listened to Mr. Trump at the New York Wealth Expo. I am a real estate investor and I think the thing I learned most from Donald was to have his attitude. I simply love his "take no nonsense" attitude. I try to think like Mr. Trump and always have that kick-ass attitude.

Thanks,

Beth Brucoli

A Bigger Purpose

After meeting and listening to Mr. Trump at The Learning Annex Wealth Expo, I found a bigger purpose in my life. I am a trained engineer and an immigrant from India. I have been investing and developing real estate for six years. I have become a multi-millionaire with properties worth over 5 million dollars, all of which I acquired and developed in just the last six years. I am now moving into Land Development. Engineering school taught me how to think creatively but Mr. Trump changed my mindset and my outlook towards life. Since the Expo, I often ask myself—Am I thinking big enough?—but more importantly, I have found a bigger purpose in my life.

Thanks & regards,

Steve Hemmady

How Donald Trump Influenced Our Lives!!!!

Hi, my name is Maria Lavoie and my husband is Joel. We live in Sudbury, Ontario, Canada. I am 41 and Joel is 38. We met 6 years ago and married in 2004. We are life and business partners.

When my husband and I attended The Learning Annex Wealth Expo in Toronto last March, we were proud of what we had accomplished thus far in our real estate endeavors, but we were still so small. We kept asking ourselves, "How do we achieve greater success?" Seeing Mr. Trump speak was life changing, but the greatest impact for us was learning to think big! Another thing that Mr. Trump taught us at The Learning Annex Wealth Expo is that you have to be passionate about what you do or you won't be successful at it. We realized our passion in real estate is that we love renovating. We love seeing the before and after! We are now flipping one house a month and our goal is to flip ten homes a month. We want to thank Donald Trump for inspiring us in so many ways. Because of his influence we are creating a grand life for ourselves! Thank you also to Bill Zanker for creating The Learning Annex Wealth Expo! It's the most exciting show we ever attended! We already have our tickets for next year! Can't wait!

Maria and Joel Lavoie

Dear Learning Annex,

Donald Trump helped me to change the way I do business. After I
attended the Wealth Expo last year my wife and I got back home in
Costa Rica and we applied Trump's advice to THINK BIG. We have
an Import and Distribution company and a Beauty Salon and Spa.
So we started thinking big, hired 3 more sales people and started
selling in all Costa Rica territory. It's now one year later and we
have two new lines that we represent, we sell 6 times what we sold
in the past and are still growing every day. We made the Beauty
Salon bigger and now we have 32 people working for us and we
signed a contract to be sponsors of the Miss Costa Rica event. We
are also opening our second Spa, Beauty Salon and Men's Club in a
big new Mall, this store is going to be 640 square meters and is
going to be on the main road of a beautiful area in San Jose. The
name of the mall MOMENTUM LINDORA has a name that
reminds me of Mr. Trump because the word Momentum he
mentioned in his books and speeches. That is the story I want to
share about how Donald Trump helped me to think big. I did and
it is great!

Thank you,

Rodrigo A. Martín

My motto is "Go Big or Go Home!" I've read all of Donald Trump's books and have learned a wealth of information from the seminars I've attended given by The Learning Annex.

In October 2004, I was on bed rest with our third child and my husband's severance package from a major music label was ending that month. I still had another five months before my child's due date; so, I had to find a way to earn an income. With no credit and no cash, I started to buy and sell properties in Buffalo, New York on eBay. The first property I bought and sold was a single family home for *only* $6,000 but from there I went on to sell over a million dollars worth of property that year. I started this business on my couch, with my laptop, the phone, and a fax machine. And I've gone on to build a very successful investment company with my husband that has branched out to include real estate investment deals in five cities total with clients all over the US, Canada, the UK, and Australia. My husband and I now have further expanded the business to include residential, mixed-use, and commercial development as well as custom home building in the booming city of Charlotte, North Carolina.

It was reading the Trump books, hearing his speeches and attending The Learning Annex's affordable yet highly informative seminars that has led to our ability to earn hundreds of thousands of dollars each year. We're not only "Thinking Big," we're "Doing Big!"

Thank you,

Nechelle and Tony Vanias
First Lady Holdings, LLC

Thanks to the Wealth Expo and Donald Trump I am going to make my first million!

I attended The Learning Annex Wealth Expo in April 2006 at the Los Angeles Convention Center. I learned so much from all the speakers those two days. However, what I learned from Trump had the biggest impact on my life. I have always believed in myself, believing that I could become rich in the real estate business. But after hearing Mr. Trump, I now feel more confident than ever. I searched through lots of property and was able to locate 160 acres that I am now in the process of subdividing into one acre lots. I will make my first million on this project, but I could not have gotten started without the confidence I gained from listening to Mr. Trump. If I had not learned to think big, I would have never taken on that big of a deal. Opportunity is endless when you open your mind. Thanks to Trump and The Learning Annex.

Shiyar Umpant

Donald's advice made my dreams come true

"If you make a decision then stick to it, keep working for it, and kick ass until you get it done." That's what I learned from Donald Trump. After reading his books and listening to him in Boston at The Learning Annex Wealth Expo, I was thrilled and excited to make my dreams become a reality. Donald's advice to change myself first, and then change my attitude in order to get to the top helped me rethink my goals, priorities and focus. His advice to keep up my momentum has been my guiding star. My dreams have come true with Donald, and he has the ability to make your dreams come true too.

Ashish Jain

The Learning Annex has changed my life!

My name is Gary Jeanty and my life changed drastically when I attended The Learning Annex Wealth Expo in Fort Lauderdale, Florida. It was more than an experience. It was a breakthrough in my life enabling me to reach new heights in my business. I started my own business in 2003 and it was financially beneficial for me, but I lacked confidence in myself when it came to helping and teaching people. After hearing these wealthy pioneers speak about their pure success and hearing how many of their students' businesses had expanded due to their teachings, they showed me what I was missing in my own business. Since hearing these amazing stories at The Learning Annex Wealth Expo, my business has grown tenfold while my real estate investing knowledge has also grown exponentially. I am also on the verge of writing a small short film on the importance of motivating yourself to higher goals. I believe none of this would have happened without Bill Zanker's vision. Bill Zanker has influenced me a great deal in my business and having people like Donald Trump, David Bach, Tony Robbins, and Paula White speak at The Learning Annex Wealth Expo has made me want to do something special in this world. Thank You, William Zanker.

Gary Jeanty

Mr. Trump YOU ROCK!!!

When I heard that Mr. Trump was speaking at The Learning Annex Wealth Expo in Philadelphia, I just had to be there. This was my chance to see him upfront and hear how he got to where he is today. So, I purchased tickets for my mother and I and went! Wow, what a weekend. I learned so much listening to Donald Trump. How he had both highs and lows and obstacles to overcome. The weekend was great motivation for me to get out there and make something of myself. He was and always will be someone to look up to for the rest of my life. I want to work hard and achieve the success that Trump has! Mr. Trump YOU ROCK!!!

Chris Offenbacker

There is no end in sight!

Donald has been one of the major motivating factors in my life, which has changed drastically since mid-2005. I basically went from a general building contractor to a builder/developer of many multimillion dollar ventures, deals, and contracts all by changing my mind-set, focus and determination to succeed. And there is no end in sight! I've read more books and studied more in the last two years than throughout my entire life. With mentors and authors such as Donald Trump, Tony Robbins, Robert Kiyosaki, Norman Vincent Peale, James Ray, Napoleon Hill, and the like, one can only rise in success and fortune. I love it!

Regards,

Anthony Pasquale, President and CEO,
Conquest Development, Inc.

Thanks for helping me learn from the best.

I have a passion for business and want to learn from the best.
When I saw Donald Trump at The Learning Annex Wealth Expo, it
opened up a whole new world for me. There was so much energy
and creativity in the room sparked by Donald and his inspirational
stories. He takes huge risks and doesn't worry about what other
people may think of him. It is because of leaders like Donald
Trump who share their stories and advice along with some great
leaders in my own career that I am able to succeed.

Sincerely,

Tammy Proctor-Blauvelt

Donald Trump's advice got me through the tough times!

Here is my story about how Donald Trump has motivated me
during my career.

I am a Real Estate Broker with my own firm in Norwood, MA.
I have been in the business for 10 years now and run a very
reputable organization. I currently staff 18 agents and although we
are a small office we produce a good volume. We usually rank in
the top 10% out of 100 offices in the South Eastern part of
Massachusetts.

Years ago I had decided to open my own firm. As I was
preparing to do so I received a phone call from a local Realtor
saying he was looking for a partner to take over half of the
ownership of two offices he had. I evaluated the situation and
thought that this would be a great opportunity for me. I would be
achieving what I started out to do in owning my own business and

more importantly, this business was already up and running. It was established and had a well recognized name world-wide. My problem then was getting the funds necessary to do this. My husband and I decided to mortgage our house to get the money. I had no doubts in my ability to work hard and I knew that with the dedication I had to my business and my clients I could succeed. For the next year and a half I helped build this company up and was proud of what we seemed to be accomplishing. My partner had always kept track of our books and finances. All seemed well until one day I suggested that we use some of our profits to pay our quarterly taxes. At this point, I had never taken any profit out of the company, only my own commissions. The silence in the room was deafening. He said "Give me a couple of weeks and maybe I can come up with a thousand or two." At that point I knew that all the hard work and faith I had put in was not for my benefit at all. It took me six months to dissolve the partnership that I had put my home on the line for.

I decided that I was not going to let this stop me. I knew I still wanted my own firm and that I could make it successful. I had less than no money, and I still had to re-pay my mortgage debt and had nothing to start a company up with. The one thing I did have was my husband's faith in me. He went and borrowed money out of his retirement fund with the agreement that it had to be paid back within the next 12 months. I knew everything was on the line now but kept my belief that with hard work I would succeed.

In 2001, I opened the doors to McNulty Realtors and until my writing of this story have never looked back. I re-paid my husband's retirement loan and my mortgage loan in the first 6 months. In my first year of business I had exceeded every goal I set for myself. In 2003 I was awarded "Businessperson of the Year" at a special presentation at the White House.

Donald Trump's advice has helped me many times along the way. It is easy to follow his guidelines in the good times, but to be honest, it was in the tough times that they helped me through the most. The one thing he always says is "Love what you do and become good at it." I have followed his career and seen the many challenges he has had to face and rise above. He has motivated me to heights I only dreamed of. I attended his Wealth Expo in Boston last year at The Learning Annex and although I didn't get to meet him I hope that one day I can thank him in person. He is a true tribute to perseverance.

Thank you for taking the time to read my story.

Sincerely,

Patty McNulty, McNulty Realtors

THE LEARNING ANNEX RECOMMENDED "MUST READS"

Bach, David. *The Automatic Millionaire: A Powerful One-Step Plan to Live and Finish Rich.* New York: Broadway Books, 2003.

Byrne, Rhonda. *The Secret.* New York: Atria Books/Beyond Words, 2006.

Collins, Jim. *Good to Great: Why Some Companies Make the Leap . . . and Others Don't.* New York: Collins, 2001.

Corbett, Michael. *Find It, Fix It, Flip It.* New York: Penguin Group, 2006.

Covey, Stephen. *Seven Habits of Highly Effective People: Power-ful Lessons in Personal Change.* New York: Simon & Schuster, 1989.

Cramer, James J. *Jim Cramer's Mad Money: Watch TV, Get Rich.* New York: Simon & Schuster, 2006.

Canfield, Jack, and Janet Switzer. *The Success Principles™: How to Get from Where You Are to Where You Want to Be.* New York: HarperCollins, 2006.

Canfield, Jack, and Mark Victor Hansen. *Chicken Soup for the Entrepreneur's Soul: Advice and Inspiration on Fulfilling Dreams.* Florida: HCI Books, 2006.

Dyer, Wayne W. *The Power of Intention.* California: Hay House, 2004.

Ferrazzi, Keith, and Tahl Raz. *Never Eat Alone: And Other Secrets to Success, One Relationship at a Time.* New York: Currency Doubleday, 2005.

Foreman, George. *George Foreman's Guide to Life: How to Get Up Off the Canvas When Life Knocks You Down.* New York: Simon & Schuster, 2002.

———. *God in My Corner: A Spiritual Memoir.* Tennessee: Thomas Nelson, 2007.

Kiyosaki, Robert, and Sharon L. Letcher. *Rich Dad, Poor Dad.* New York: Warner Business Books, 2000.

Langemeier, Loral. *The Millionaire Maker's Guide to Creating a*

Cash Machine for Life. New York: McGraw-Hill 1 edition, 2007.

Orman, Suze. *Women & Money: Owning the Power to Control Your Destiny*. New York: Doubleday Spiegel & Grau, 2007.

Robbins, Anthony. *Awaken the Giant Within: How to Take Control of Your Mental, Emotional, Physical & Financial Destiny!* New York: Simon & Schuster, 1992.

———. *Unlimited Power: The New Science Of Personal Achievement*. New York: Simon & Schuster, 1997.

Ross, George H. *Trump-Style Negotiation: Powerful Strategies and Tactics for Mastering Every Deal*. Indiana: Wiley Publishing, Inc., 2006.

Schragis, Steven. *10 Clowns Don't Make a Circus: And 249 Other Critical Management Success Strategies*. Ohio: Adams Media Corporation, 2006.

Shemin, Robert. *How Come That Idiot's Rich and I'm Not?* New York: Crown Publisher's, 2007.

Simmons, Russell. *Do You!: 12 Laws to Access the Power in You to Achieve Happiness and Success*. New York: Penguin Group's Gotham, 2007.

Tolle, Eckhart. *The Power of Now: A Guide to Spiritual Enlightenment*. California: New World Library, 2004.

Trump, Donald J., and Tony Schwartz. *Trump: The Art of the Deal*. New York: Random House, 1 edition, 1987.

Trump, Donald J., Meredith McIver. *Trump 101: The Way to Success.* New Jersey: Wiley Publishing, Inc., 2006.

Welch, Jack. *Winning.* New York: HarperBusiness Publishers, 2005.

White, Paula. *You're All That!: Understand God's Design for Your Life.* Tennessee: Faith Words, 2007.

This is just a partial list of recommended books—for a complete listing visit LearningAnnex.com.

The Learning Annex

The Learning Annex Featured Teachers
Partial listing

Actors
*Dan Aykroyd, *Saturday Night Live*
*Jason Alexander, *Seinfeld*
*Kevin Bacon, *Footloose*
*Annette Bening, *American Beauty*
*Jessica Biel, *The Illusionist*
*Wayne Brady, *Whose Line Is It Anyway?*
*Pierce Brosnan, *Goldeneye*
*Kirk Douglas, *Spartacus*
*Tim Daly, ABC's *Eyes*, *Wings*
*Richard Dreyfuss, *Jaws*
*David Duchovney, *X Files*
*Sally Field, *Steel Magnolias*
*Harrison Ford, *Raiders of the Lost Ark*
*Charlton Heston, *The Ten Commandments*
*Val Kilmer, *The Doors*
*Jerry Lewis, *The King of Comedy*
*Sarah Jessica Parker, *Sex and the City*
*Edward Norton, *Fight Club*
*Molly Ringwald, *The Breakfast Club*
*Tim Robbins, *The Shawshank Redemption*
*Doris Roberts, *Everybody Loves Raymond*
*William Shatner, *Star Trek*
*Martin Short, *Saturday Night Live*
*Henry Winkler, *Happy Days*
*Renee Zellweger, *Chicago*

Authors
*Isaac Asimov, science fiction legend (d)
*David Baldacci, *Hour Game*
*Barbara Taylor Bradford, *A Woman Of Substance*
*Ray Bradbury, *Fahrenheit 451*
*Candace Bushnell, *Sex and the City*
*James Ellroy, *L.A. Confidential*
*Betty Friedan, *The Feminine Mystique* (d)
*Spalding Gray, *Monster in a Box* (d)
*Winston Groom, *Forrest Gump*
*Joseph Heller, *Catch-22* (d)
*Mary Higgins Clark, *Where Are the Children*
*Norman Mailer, *The Naked and the Dead*
*Frances Mayes, *Under the Tuscan Sun*
*M. Scott Peck, *The Road Less Traveled*

*Sidney Sheldon, *The Other Side of* (d)
*Amy Tan, *The Joy Luck Club*
*Kurt Vonnegut, Jr., *Slaughterhouse Five* (d)

Business/Finance/Real Estate
*Raymond Aaron, *Double Your Income Doing What You Love*
*Robert Allen, *Creating Wealth*
*David Bach, *Automatic Millionaire*
*Sir Richard Branson, *The Virgin Group*
*Richard Bolles, *What Color is Your Parachute?*
*Mark Burnett, producer, *The Apprentice*
*Don Burnham, real estate investor
*John Casablancas, Elite Modeling
*Michael Coles, CEO, Caribou Coffee
*Barbara Corcoran, real estate entrepreneur
*Mark Cuban, founder, Broadcast.com
*James Cramer, co-founder, TheStreet.com
*Donny Deutsch, CNBC's *The Big Idea*
*Steve Forbes, CEO, *Forbes* magazine
*George Foreman, entrepreneur, "The Grill"
*Jane Friedman, president/CEO, HarperCollins
*Jeffrey Gitomer, *The Little Red Book of Selling*
*Lizzie Grubman, Lizzie Grubman Public Relations
*Dottie Herman, CEO, Douglas Elliman Real Estate
*Patrick James, Tax Secrets of the Millionaires™
*Chris Johnson, InvesterWealth™
*Ron LeGrand, *How to Be a Quick Turn Real Estate Millionaire*
*Al Lowry, *How You Can Become Financially Independent by Investing in Real Estate*
*Horst M. Rechelbacher, founder, Aveda
*Bruce Karatz, CEO, KB Homes
*Robert Kiyosaki, *Rich Dad, Poor Dad* series
*Wing Lam, founder/CEO, Wahoo's Tacos
*Albert Lowry, *Formulas for Wealth*
*Harvey Mackay, *Swim with the Sharks*
*Armando Montelongo, *Flip and Grow Rich*
*David Neeleman, CEO, Jet Blue
*Craig Newmark, founder, Craigslist.com
*Suze Orman, *The 9 Steps to Financial Freedom*

*Pete Peterson, The Blackstone Group
*Anita Roddick, founder, The Body Shop
*George Ross, co-star, *The Apprentice*
*Robert Shemin, *Secrets of Buying and Selling Real Estate*
*Russell Simmons, founder, Def Jam Records
*Donald Trump, billionaire real estate developer
*Mel Ziegler, founder, Banana Republic

Directors

*Andrew Adamson, *Shrek 1 & 2, Chronicles of Narnia*
*James Burrows, *Will & Grace, Cheers*
*Frank Darabont, *The Shawshank Redemption*
*Marc Forster, *Finding Neverland*
*Terry Gilliam, *Monty Python*
*Marshall Herskovitz, *My So-Called Life*
*Ron Howard, *A Beautiful Mind*
*Gordon Hunt, *Frasier, Mad About You*
*Michael Lembeck, *Friends*
*Sidney Lumet, *12 Angry Men, The Verdict*
*Garry Marshall, *Pretty Woman*
*Brett Ratner, *Rush Hour* Series
*Gary Ross, *Seabiscuit*
*Thomas Schlamme, *The West Wing*
*Joel Schumacher, *The Phantom of the Opera*
*Adam Shankman, *Bringing Down the House*
*Ron Shelton, *Bull Durham*

Fashion/Beauty

*Carol Alt, model
*Michelle Bohbot, founder, Bisou Bisou
*Naomi Campbell, model
*Paul Charron, CEO, *Liz Claiborne*
*Kenneth Cole, shoe designer
*Kyan Douglas, *Queer Eye for the Straight Guy*
*Patricia Field, costume designer, *Sex and the City*
*Diane Von Furstenberg, designer
*Betsey Johnson, designer
*Tommy Hilfiger, designer
*Harry Langdon, celebrity photographer
*Elle Macpherson, model/actress
*Steve Madden, shoe designer
*Cynthia Rowley, designer
*Ivana Trump, founder, Ivana Haute Couture
*Vendela, model/actress
*Doug Wilson, designer, *Trading Spaces*

Fitness/Health/Nutrition

*Baron Baptiste, *Journey Into Power*
*Billy Blanks, creator of Tae-Bo
*Anne Louise Gittleman, *The Fat Flush Plan*
*Tony Little, America's Personal Trainer™
*Dr. Christine Northrup, *Women's Bodies, Women's Wisdom*
*Gary Null, *Power Aging*
*Dr. Judith Orloff, *Second Sight, Intuitive Healing*
*Dr. Dean Ornish, *Eat More, Weigh Less*
*Dr. Barry Sears, *The Zone Diet*
*Dr. Andrew Weil, *Spontaneous Healing, Eight Weeks to Optimum Health*

Music

*Judy Collins, singer
*Sean "Diddy" Combs, Bad Boy Entertainment
*Damon Dash, co-CEO, Roc-A-Fella Records
*Chaka Khan, 8-time Grammy-winner
*Clive Davis, chairman, SONY BMG North America
*John Densmore, The Doors
* Peter Frampton, singer
*Marvin Hamlisch, composer, *A Chorus Line*
*Mickey Hart, The Grateful Dead
*Naomi Judd, singer
*Mathew Knowles, manager, Beyonce
*Lisa Loeb, singer
*Ray Manzarek, The Doors
*Wynton Marsalis, jazz musician
*Alannis Morrisette, singer
*Nile Rodgers, founder, Chic
*Bernie Taupin, songwriter, Grammy-winner
*Steven Van Zandt, The E Street Band
*Max Weinberg, The E Street Band
*Ron Wood, guitarist, The Rolling Stones

Personal Growth/Relationships

*Martha Beck, *Find Your True North Star, Expecting Adam,* columnist for *O* magazine
*Rev. Michael Beckwith, founder, Agape Spiritual Center
*Rhonda Britten, *Change Your Life in 30 Days*
*Erin Brockovich-Ellis, *Challenge America with Erin Brockovich*
*Les Brown, *Live Full and Die Empty*
*Julia Cameron, *The Artist's Way*
*Jack Canfield, *Chicken Soup for the Soul*
*Jean Chatzky, *Make Money Not Excuses*
*Dr. Deepak Chopra, *The Seven Spiritual Laws of Success*

*Ram Dass, *Be Here Now*
*Dr. Barbara De Angelis, *Secrets About Men Every Woman Should Know*
*John DeMartini, *You Can Have an Amazing Life in Just 60 Days*
*Hale Dwoskin, *The Sedona Method*
*John Edward, *Afterlife*
*Dr. Wayne Dyer, *Your Erroneous Zones*
*Kathy Freston, *Expect a Miracle*
*Stedman Graham, *You Can Make it Happen*
*John Gray, *Men are from Mars, Women are from Venus*
*Mark Victor Hansen, *Chicken Soup for the Soul*
*David Hawkins, *Power vs. Force*
*Dr. Ben Johnson, featured in *The Secret*
*Loral Langemeier, *The Millionaire Maker*
*Dan Millman, featured in *The Secret*
*Lisa Nichols, featured in *The Secret*
*James Redfield, *The Celestine Prophecy*
*Tony Robbins, success coach, bestselling author
*James Ray, featured in *The Secret*
*Don Miguel Ruiz, *The Four Agreements*
*David Schirmer, featured in *The Secret*
*Dr. Laura Schlessinger, national radio personality
*Marci Shimoff, *Chicken Soup for the Mother's Soul*
*Dr. Bernie Siegel, *Love, Medicine and Miracles*
*Eckhart Tolle, *The Power of Now*
*Marianne Williamson, *Return to Love*
*Iyanla Vanzant, life coach on *Starting Over*
*Dennis Waitley, *The Subliminal Winner*
*Paula White, *Becoming a Millionaire God's Way*
*Gary Zukav, *The Seat of the Soul*

Politics
*Barbara Bush, former First Lady of the United States
*Bill Clinton, former President of the United States
*Mario Cuomo, former Governor of New York
*Rudy Giuliani, former Mayor of New York City
*Al Gore, former Vice-President of the United States
*Alan Greenspan, former Federal Reserve Chairman of the United States
*Abbie Hoffman, political activist (d)
*Arianna Huffington, political commentator
*Henry Kissinger, former Secretary of State for the United States
*Ed Koch, former Mayor of New York City

*Jerry Rubin, political activist (d)
*Bishop Desmond Tutu, recipient of the Nobel Peace Prize
*Jesse Ventura, former Governor of Minnesota

Restaurant/Food Industry
*Wally Amos, Famous Amos Cookies
*Ben Cohen, Ben & Jerry's Ice Cream
*Rosie Daley, *In the Kitchen with Rosie*
*Rocco DiSpirito, *The Restaurant*
*Faith Stewart Gordon, The Russian Tea Room (d)
*Tim Zagat, founder, Zagat Survey

Screenwriting
*Allison Anders, *Gas, Food, Lodging*
*Syd Field, author, script consultant
*Larry Gelbart, *Tootsie, Oh, God!, M*A*S*H*
*Akiva Goldsmith, *Cinderella Man, Da Vinci Code*
*Lew Hunter, author, script consultant
*Robert McKee, author, script consultant
*Gary Ross, *Pleasantville, Seabiscuit*
*Ellen Sandler, *Everybody Loves Raymond*

Showbiz/Media
*Peter Bart, editor-in-chief, *Variety*, co-host, *Sunday Morning Shoot-Out*
*Bernie Brillstein, founder, Brillstein-Grey Management
*John Cooper, director, Sundance Film Festival
*Debra Curtis, vice-president, SONY Pictures TV
*Robert Evans, producer, *The Godfather*
*Karen Foster, executive, Dreamworks Animation
*Christian Gaines, director, American Film Institute Festivals
*Jon Gordon, co-president of production, Miramax
*Jeff Gorin, agent, William Morris Agency
*Peter Guber, co-host of *Sunday Morning Shoot-Out*
*Steven Haft, producer, *Dead Poet's Society*
*Madelyn Hammond, associate publisher, *Variety*; editor, *V-Life* magazine
*Arthur Hiller, president, Academy of Motion Picture Arts & Sciences
*Jeff Howard, executive, DisneyToon Studios
*Larry Hummell, agent, International Creative Management
*Stan Lee, creator of Spider-man, X-Men, The Incredible Hulk
*Dave Mace, vice-president, Storyline Entertainment, *Chicago*

*Lynda Obst, producer, *Sleepless in Seattle*
*Richard Masur, president, Screen Actors Guild
*Eric Poticha, vice-president, Jim Henson
Company
*Arnold Rifkin, former head, William Morris
Agency
*Natanya Rose, agent, William Morris Agency
*Stan Rosenfield,.celebrity publicist
*Harvey Weinstein, president, Miramax Films
*David Wirtschafter, worldwide head of motion
pictures, William Morris Agency

Spirituality/Psychics/Intuitives
*Sylvia Browne, *The Other Side and Back*
*John Edward, *One Last Time*
*Dr. Masuru Emoto, *The Hidden Messages
in Water*
*Uri Geller, world-renowned psychic
*Caroline Myss, *Anatomy of the Spirit*
*Judith Orloff, *Second Sight*
*Don Miguel Ruiz, *The Four Agreements*
*James Van Praagh, *Talking to Heaven*
*Dr. Brian Weiss, *Many Lives, Many Masters*

Sports
*Kareem Abdul Jabaar, NBA Hall-of-Famer
*Tiki Barber, New York Giants, broadcaster
*Dr J, Julius Erving, NBA Hall-of-Famer
* Walt Frazier, NBA Hall-of-Famer
*Phil Hellmuth, Jr., 9-time World Poker Champion
* Earvin Magic Johnson, NBA Hall-of-Famer
*Al Leiter, pitcher, New York Mets
*John McEnroe, world class tennis player
*Omar Minaya, general manager, New York Mets
*Earl Monroe, NBA Hall-of-Famer
*Joe Montana, quarterback NFL Hall-of-Famer
*Norm Nixon, former Los Angeles Laker
*Leigh Steinberg, famed sports attorney

*Joe Torre, manager, New York Yankees
*Bill Walsh, coach, San Francisco 49ers (d)
*Dominique Wilkins, NBA Hall-of-Famer

Television Personalities
*Ellen DeGeneres, comedian, *The Ellen
DeGeneres Show*
*Kyan Douglas, *Queer Eye for the Straight Guy*
*Daniel Franco, *Project Runway* Seasons 1 & 2
*Maria Bartiromo, anchor, CNBC
*Andrae Gonzalo, *Project Runway* Season 2
*Kathy Griffin, actress and comedian
*Larry King, talk show host, *Larry King Live*
*Star Jones, TV Personality
*Matt Lauer, co-anchor, *The Today Show*
*Jay McCarroll, winner, *Project Runway* Season 1
*Kelly Perdew, winner, *The Apprentice*
*Regis Philbin, talk show host, *Live with Regis
and Kelly*
*David Price, CBS News
*Joan Rivers, comedian
*Jai Rodriguez, *Queer Eye for the Straight Guy*
*Al Roker, *The Today Show*
*Joel Siegel, film critic, *Good Morning America* (d)
*Jerry Springer, talk show host, *The Jerry
Springer Show*

(d) indicates deceased

This is a partial list of more than
30,000 experts, leaders, thinkers
and doers who have taught and
inspired students at The Learning
Annex since 1980. If you would like
to teach at The Learning Annex,
upload your one minute video at
www.OneMinuteU.com.

ACKNOWLEDGMENTS FROM DONALD J. TRUMP

Working with Bill Zanker and his team at The Learning Annex has been a great pleasure. My experience as a speaker with them prepared me for the professional and enthusiastic approach we had in writing this book together. Many thanks to Bill, Heather Moore, and all of the wonderful people at The Learning Annex.

I'd like to thank my front office team at The Trump Organization, especially my chief assistant, Rhona Graff, my staff writer, Meredith McIver, and Kacey Kennedy in media relations. Your hard work and diligence is greatly appreciated.

ACKNOWLEDGMENTS FROM DONALD J. TRUMP

HarperCollins has done a terrific job and I'd like to thank Jane Friedman, CEO; Steve Ross, President of Collins; Ethan Friedman, Editor; Margot Schupf, Group Sr. Vice President & Associate Publisher; Josh Marwell, President of Sales; Angie Lee, Marketing Director; Paul Olsewski, Senior Director of Publicity; Laurence Hughes, Director of Publicity; Felicia Sullivan, Senior Online Marketing Manager; and Richard Ljoenes, Art Director. Your work has been excellent on all levels, and I'm pleased to have had this opportunity to work with such a fine group. I have had many #1 bestsellers but this is the best of them all.

Donald J. Trump

ACKNOWLEDGMENTS FROM BILL ZANKER

What an honor to write a book with my own personal hero, Donald Trump. It has been so exciting! Rhona Graff, Donald's main assistant is such a pleasure to work with. Being straightforward, hard-working and honest makes working with Donald easy. Everyone else at The Trump Organization is just great. When I visit Donald in his office, I get goose bumps. Even though I have visited him often, it is always extraordinary and I learn something new every time. The day before I am going to meet him, I can hardly sleep. I get so excited. Thank you Donald for taking me into your life.

The Learning Annex is an amazing company. But a company is really just people, and I want to especially thank my top executives. Heather Moore who took ownership of this book while the rest of us continued to make magic happen in other parts of the company . . . Samantha Del Canto, Harry Javer, Paul Gould, Michele D'Agostino, Oliver Waller, Jessie Schwartzburg, Morris Orens, Andy Hyams, and Stephen Seligman. I also want to thank Steven Schragis, Theo Bartek, Amy Deneson, Terry Derkach, Emily Kozlow, and John Christmas for doing what they do best. We are a small group of executives for the amount of business we do, but we have an unbelievable organization behind us of over 100 strong Kick Ass employees who always say, "Yes." I adore my team. And I share their passion.

Larry Kirshbaum is the agent for this book. I knew him when he was President of Time Warner Books. He is now an entrepreneur with his own literary agency, LJK Literary. I told him I wanted a publisher who had a Think Big attitude and could get the book out quickly. He said no problem, and within a week we had a deal with one of the largest and best publishers in the world . . . Collins. Wow! And the people there were great . . . all with Kick Ass attitudes. Thanks to Steve Ross, the President of Collins who understood what this book was all about immediately and a big thank you to his team with special kudos to Ethan.

Larry Kirshbaum . . . thank you and welcome to The Learning Annex team as our new book agent. I love seeing a big shot corporate guy like you become an entrepreneur. You're our type of Kick-Ass agent.

Lastly, I need to thank all my teachers at The Learning Annex who have taught and inspired me and my students for almost thirty years. Recently, Hollywood legend Peter Guber has been personally mentoring me, and I am so grateful for his help. We all need coaches at different times in our lives, and Peter is thought provoking and brilliant. He shares my passion of learning from the great minds. Tony Robbins has re-energized my life on so many occasions. He brings a shining light and joy to the world. I only hope he knows how much he has helped me and millions of others day in and day out. Thank you Tony for being Tony and never compromising your mission and passion.

There have been so many other teachers that have gotten me to laugh, cry, re-evaluate my life, get it back on course, change my direction, improve my relationship with my wife, my children, my friends, my G-d, and myself. I thank you all for your passion in serving us, your students. I meet many of my teachers as they are on their mission to help people, and I can't applaud them enough. I watch as they roll into town after town, sleeping in nondescript hotel rooms, all for the chance to help one more student. I love you, and I thank you for all you do. You are the greatest gift to the world.

Bill Zanker

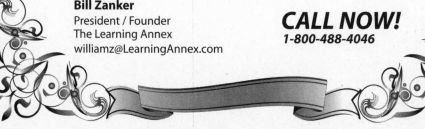

INDEX

INDEX

Hill, Napoleon, 340
Hinneberg family, 95
hiring, 154–58, 166, 175, 176, 305–6
Hollywood, 28
honesty, 156
Hornblower, Josiah, 67
Howard, 261
Hyams, Adam, 170–71

Iacocca, Lee, 145–47
Icahn, Carl, 107
idea people, 46
Inc., 98
India, 334
Inside Edition (TV show), 188
Intel, 92
interest rates, 156–57, 306, 316
Iran, 152, 153, 205, 277
Iraq War, 61
IT quality, 16–22, 37
ITT, 204, 205–6

Jain, Ashish, 338
Jamaica, 167
Jarvis, Rebecca, 160–61
Javer, Harry, 172
Javits Center, 23
Jeanty, Gary, 339
Jennifer, 257–58
Jersey City, N.J., 289
Jerusalem College of Technology, 298
Jeter, Derek, 56, 267
Jimmy Carter Library, 277
Jobs, Steve, 46, 132
John, Elton, 140
Jolie, Angelina, 273
Jones Beach, 321–22, 327
Jordan, Michael, 267

Kabatznik, Clive, 169–70
Kepcher, Carolyn, 232–34
King, Larry, 120, 255

Kiyosaki, Robert, 219, 340
Klein, Murray, 34–35
Koch, Ed, 243–44
Kraft, Bob, 281, 310
Kravis, Henry, 107

La Belle Simone (yacht), 205
Lachey, Nick, 259
Langemeier, Loral, 220
Larry King Live (TV show), 220
Lashley, Bobby, 121
Las Vegas, Nev., 115, 254
Lavoie, Maria and Joel, 335
Learning Annex, 33, 74–75, 195–96
    catalog of, 244
    channel of, 244–45
    chief financial officer of, 169–70
    Empire State Building money drop
        of, 129–31, 219
    featured teachers of, 349–52
    Hyams at, 170–71
    imitation of, 194–95
    Kiyosaki at, 36
    Klein at, 34–35
    reading recommendations of,
        345–48
    repurchase of, 98–99
    start of, 73–74, 96, 296
    testimonials on, 329–43
    Trump at, 42, 97, 131, 151–52, 219,
        244, 257–58, 282–83
    Wealth Expo, 42, 126, 131–32, 167,
        168, 219, 244, 245, 299, 316
Lechter, Sharon, 35–36
Lerner, Al, 292
Levitt, William, 203–7, 212
Lincoln Center, 292
Liston, Sonny, 279
Los Angeles, Calif., 62, 65, 239, 244
Los Angeles Convention Center, 338
Los Angeles Times, 220
Lowe, Rob, 87
loyalty, 156–61, 171, 176, 308

INDEX

INDEX

INDEX

YOURS FREE!
2 Tickets (Worth $358)
To See a *Learning Annex WEALTH EXPO* Near You.

Dear Reader,

You have taken the first step in Thinking BIG and Kicking Ass
by reading this book. Now you can get a shot of caffeine to jump-start your new think-big-kick-
ass attitude fast.

It's called the *Learning Annex WEALTH EXPO*. Dozens of the world's most powerful peak performance and financial experts will spend two full days training and inspiring you to enter into the super-charged mindset of extraordinary achievers.

Two tickets normally cost $358 ($179 each)...But these two tickets are yours free when you purchase my book with Donald Trump, *Think Big and Kick Ass in Business and Life*, published by HarperCollins.

The *Learning Annex WEALTH EXPO* is a Boot Camp for
Big Thinkers.

I absolutely believe that a sudden event in anyone's life can trigger a MASSIVE CHANGE...a gigantic attitude shift where everything is different, everything is better...and you are doing the things and making the money you've always wanted to make. I've personally seen this happen over and over again...

That is why I created the **WEALTH EXPO** and hired super-successful powerhouse peak performance speakers like **Tony Robbins, Donald Trump, George Foreman** and the stars of *The Secret* including: **Jack Canfield, Loral Langemeier** and **Lisa Nichols** to give you a jolt of energy to propel you to a new and prosperous chapter in your life. More featured speakers are added all the time!*

Accept this invitation now, and let the **Expo** shake you out of your rut, and motivate you to take action **now** to realize your dreams, your goals and your hopes for financial security, and the freedom to do whatever you want in life. A year from now you will look back at today as the day YOUR WHOLE LIFE TURNED AROUND!

All You Need to Do is Walk Through the Door and the Expo
"Magic" Will Work Its Wonders on YOU!

The **Expo** will leave you exhilarated, with a new sense of purpose and determination that you have never had before...to start your own business, create a second income in real estate, in the stock market, in an internet business, or in one of the dozens of other business education opportunities that are proven money machines.

Our teachers are super-successful "millionaire makers" who will expand your horizons to a level you never thought possible!

Now it's time to take action by attending a FREE *Learning Annex WEALTH*
EXPO in your area

Your first step is easy. Just register now. It costs you nothing. A Full Weekend Pass to the **WEALTH EXPO** regularly costs $179*. But you will not pay $179 for it...If you register now, you receive two Full Weekend Passes FREE, when you purchase my book with Donald Trump, *Think Big and Kick Ass in Business and Life*.

Some of what you'll learn about:

- **17 businesses you can start NOW**
- Finding, funding & selling foreclosures
- **New tax laws regarding capital gains & recapture of depreciation**
- Becoming an eBay entrepreneur
- **Strategies to improve poor credit scores**
- How to use existing IRA or 401K dollars to buy multiple properties
- **Sales secrets of the selling superstars**
- Think and be rich
- **Mortgages - Locking in the lowest rate & negotiating the best terms**

- **Legal steps necessary to protect your business and ideas**
- Identifying the right markets to invest in
- **How to invest in multiple markets across the country at the same time**
- Raising private money the fast & easy way
- **Building an instant Internet marketing plan**
- Low cost/no cost techniques to instantly get new business
- **What are the right investments?**
- How to prepare sales forecasts and financial statements
- **Real estate profits with no money down**
- And much, much more!

A New American Millionaire is Born Every 24 Seconds
Now IT'S YOUR TIME

In past years there have been people who attended the **Expo** who went on to become millionaires. Now it's YOUR TIME to experience what it's like to think bigger and live bigger than you've ever imagined. Once you get a taste of the rich life, you will <u>never</u> want to turn back!

Call **right now** to register. <u>Five minutes</u> is all it takes...It's a <u>small step</u> that could make you millions. Call **1-800-488-0846** in North America or register online at ThinkBIGseminars.com

Warmly,

Bill Zanker

Bill Zanker
President/Founder
The Learning Annex
williamz@LearningAnnex.com

P.S. A Full Weekend Pass to **The Learning Annex WEALTH EXPO** regularly costs $179*. But you will **not** pay $179 for it...Two Full Weekend Passes, a $358 value, are **yours free** while supplies last. Seating is limited and available on a first-come, first-serve basis. **Register now to avoid disappointment.**

THE LEARNING ANNEX
FREE EXPO TICKET CERTIFICATE

Bill Zanker invites you and a family member to a
Learning Annex WEALTH EXPO in your area.
To register and to get more information, go to
www.ThinkBIGSeminars.com

If you prefer to talk to a representative, please call
Call **1-800-488-0846** in North America.
International callers use **646-346-2905**

Use your book receipt # _____ when you register

* Offer open to purchasers of Think Big and Kick Ass by Donald Trump and Bill Zanker. Original proof of purchase may be required. Pre-registration required, by going to ThinkBigSeminars.com. Seating is limited and available on first-come first-serve basis. Retail value of $358 is based on admission price at the door as of August 29, 2007. Groups may not use one book purchase for admission of more than two people. Attendees are responsible for their own travel costs. The Learning Annex may refuse admission to anyone who it believes will interfere with others' enjoyment of the program. Speakers subject to change and not all speakers in all locations. See additional rules and expiration date on website ThinkBigSeminars.com.